# Remembrance Book

# Remembrance Book

Carol Gura

Rita Ferrone

Steve Lanza

Bob Duggan

Gael Gensler

Donna Steffen

*RITE OF CHRISTIAN INITIATION OF ADULTS*

RCL Benziger®

Cincinnati, Ohio

ROMAN MISSAL
THIRD EDITION

Nihil Obstat
Rev. Msgr. Glenn D. Gardner, J.C.D.
Censor Librorum

Imprimatur
† Most Rev. Charles V. Grahmann
Bishop of Dallas

October 19, 1998

The Nihil Obstat and Imprimatur are official declarations that the material reviewed is free of doctrinal or moral error. No implication is contained therein that those granting the Nihil Obstat and Imprimatur agree with the contents, opinions, or statements expressed.

Send all inquiries to:
RCL Benziger
8805 Governor's Hill Drive • Suite 400
Cincinnati, Ohio 45249

Toll free    877-275-4725
Fax          800-688-8356

Visit us at www.RCLBenziger.com

Printed in the United States of America

**12714**    ISBN 978-0-7829-0768-1

10th Printing. January 2015.

# Table of Contents

# Introduction

*D*ear Catechumen and Candidate,

*W*elcome to a most exciting and momentous journey. Your willingness to follow God's call and enter into full communion with the People of God in the Catholic faith is important and significant. The faith of Catholics is deepened and enhanced by your presence and openness to the Rite of Christian Initiation of Adults process. Thus, we commit ourselves to be present with you throughout this journey and to be open to receive the transformative presence of God's Spirit with and through you.

The *Remembrance Book* is designed to help you on this journey. It begins with "Significant People and Special Moments," a space designated to keep a record of the important people and moments along this initiation journey. This journey of faith consists in a twofold movement. The inner passage to uncover the wellspring of God's triune presence within occurs simultaneously with an outward movement to embrace the rich treasure of the Catholic community of faith. Meditation on the liturgical seasons of the Church year provides the framework for this dual process of conversion. In the section "Journeying through the Seasons," inspirational poems, prayers, and writings by a variety of authors are offered for each week throughout the year to help you reflect on the depths of God's transforming action in your life. Short descriptions of the lives of the Saints are interjected throughout the seasons of the Church year in order that you might encounter examples of real people whose lives model Gospel living. As you mark the various steps along this initiation process, "Steps on the Journey" offers opportunities to reflect upon the various liturgical rites and, ultimately, the sacramental encounter of the living Christ in Baptism, Confirmation, and Eucharist. In the section "Treasures of the Catholic Tradition," the richness of Catholic prayer and the faith tradition are presented.

This book is a remembrance of your faith journey into the community of the Catholic Church. Use it to write about your insights and struggles and the significant people you encounter as you integrate this process into your life. Share the thoughts, questions, and experiences gleaned through these reflections with your sponsor and other significant spiritual companions. Take some quiet time each week to reflect upon the meditation provided; carry it with you as you go about your ordinary life's work. You may choose to record your thoughts and reflections each week, in other words, to keep a journal of your growth in this process. We suggest that you acquire a special journaling book or tablet for this purpose. Throughout the year read about the Saints whose feasts are celebrated and follow through with a resolve to imitate their lives. Refer to the traditional prayers and try them out on a daily basis as you seek a deeper relationship with the Lord and the People of God. It is important that you make this book your own. Use it in ways that fit your lifestyle and integrate the treasury of the spiritual life presented here into your life.

As we all seek to conform to Christ, we walk together on this mutual journey of conversion. Our focus is to allow the Spirit to transform us that we might become a new creation in Christ. We, the members of the Catholic family, offer our prayers and our stories of faith as we accompany you on this journey. May we all be changed, healed, and united as we clothe ourselves in Christ. In the words of Saint Paul, we pray "that, according to the riches of his glory, he may grant that you may be strengthened in your inner being with power through his Spirit, and that Christ may dwell in your hearts through faith, as you are being rooted and grounded in love. I pray that you may have the power to comprehend, with all the saints, what is the breadth and length and height and depth, and to know the love of Christ that surpasses knowledge, so that you may be filled with all the fullness of God" (Ephesians 3:16–19).

That we all may be one in Christ,

The Writing Team

# Journeying through the Seasons

# The Season of Advent

# Advent

The beginning of the Church's new year
is birthed in darkness. The light of day grows short.
In the lengthening night we cry out,
prisoners of the past,
comfortable in what is known.
It is not easy leaving aside the old.
Endings and the end things
are always frightening.
In the darkness and shadows
we face our deepest fears.
Wondering,
watching,
waiting,
we hold on in hope.

This old year must give way
to the new, the unknown.
This year,
this time,
will the dawn slip across the horizon?

For, in the rising sun,
the light is born, shattering the dark.
In the morning, light our hearts,
stretch to grasp the new.

Then the full light of the Son
will reveal this is not the end—
only another beginning.

Carol A. Gura

*Saints for the Season*

DECEMBER 3: SAINT FRANCIS XAVIER (1506–1552) is considered one of the greatest Christian missionaries. Francis was a companion to Saint Ignatius of Loyola in founding the Society of Jesus. His work in India with the lower caste and later in Japan won him the title "patron of foreign missions." Today think about your openness to those who are different, poor, or from another country.

# THE SECOND COMING
### C. S. Lewis

In *King Lear* (III: vii) there is a man who is such a minor character that Shakespeare has not given him even a name: he is merely "First Servant." All the characters around him—Regan, Cornwall, and Edmund—have fine, long-term plans. They think they know how the story is going to end, and they are quite wrong. The servant has no such delusions. He has no notion how the play is going to go. But he understands the present scene. He sees an abomination (the blinding of old Gloucester) taking place. He will not stand it. His sword is out and pointed at his master's breast in a moment: then Regan stabs him dead from behind. That is his whole part: eight lines all told. But if it were real life and not a play, that is the part it would be best to have acted.

The doctrine of the Second Coming teaches us that we do not and cannot know when the world drama will end. The curtain may be rung down at any moment: say, before you have finished reading this paragraph. This seems to some people intolerably frustrating. So many things would be interrupted. Perhaps you were going to get married next month, perhaps you were going to get a raise next week: you may be on the verge of a great scientific discovery: you may be maturing great social and political reforms. Surely no good and wise God would be so very unreasonable as to cut all this short? Not now, of all moments!

But we think thus because we keep on assuming that we know the play. We do not know the play. We do not even know whether we are in Act I or Act V. The Author knows. The audience, if there is an audience (if angels and archangels and all the company of Heaven fill the pit and the stalls), may have an inkling. But we, never seeing the play from outside, never meeting the characters except the tiny minority who are "on" in the same scenes as ourselves, wholly ignorant of the future and very imperfectly informed about the past, cannot tell at what moment the end ought to come. That it will come when it ought, we may be sure; but we waste our time in guessing when that will be. That it has a meaning we may be sure, but we cannot see it. When it is over, we may be told. We are led to expect that the Author will have something to say to each of us on the part that each of us has played. The playing it well is what matters infinitely.

The doctrine of the Second Coming, then, is not to be rejected because it conflicts with our favorite modern mythology. It is, for that very reason, to be the more valued and made more frequently the subject of meditation. It is the medicine our condition especially needs.

 *Saints for the Season*

DECEMBER 4: SAINT JOHN OF DAMASCUS (ca. 675–749), an Arab Christian, was a Doctor of the Church and a Greek theologian. After ministering to the caliphs, like his father and grandfather, he retired to the monastery of Saint Sabas, where he was ordained a priest and wrote many notable theological treatises. John is especially noted for his works on the real presence of Christ in the Eucharist and for his Marian belief in the Immaculate Conception and the Assumption of Mary into Heaven. Today read a section of a theological book you have at hand.

# MARY

*George R. Szews*

The poor, lowly, simple, and desperate have always had a special love for Mary.

A dime-store psychologist might say it's because people are always looking for the mother who feeds them and tells them everything will be OK. A cynic and chauvinist might say it's because mothers always give in and most people are afraid that, even though Jesus called God *Abba,* God will really turn out to be the disciplinarian of the family.

Women and men of faith, however, who have fled to Mary for help, cried to her on their pillows and clung to her image for protection, believe Mary knows something about the heart of God. Mary's song is her hope and her hope leaves little beads of sweat on the brows of the mighty while it makes bearable this vale of tears for the left out and troubled.

Mary makes life bearable for the poorest of the poor and the poor who haven't enough sense to know they're poor. Mary puts life in perspective for the haughty and powerful who know someday they'll have to pay the piper, and those lost in between conceit and simplicity who profess Christianity because everybody does. Mary even makes life on earth possible for God who found in her enough courage to keep going no matter what and enough hope to believe she couldn't do it on her own.

 *Saints for the Season*

*DECEMBER 6: SAINT NICHOLAS* (d. ca. 350), patron of sailors and children, is the original Santa Claus. Nicholas, bishop of Myra, was noted for his holiness and pastoral zeal. After his death, many legends of his healing miracles and generosity became widely known. Today give the gift of your time and presence to someone in need.

# ADVENT HOPE
*Henri Nouwen*

"A shoot shall sprout from the stump of Jesse, and from his roots a bud shall blossom. The spirit of the LORD shall rest upon him . . ." (Isaiah 11:1–2).

These words from last night's liturgy have stayed with me during the day. Our salvation comes from something small, tender, and vulnerable, something hardly noticeable. God, who is the Creator of the Universe, comes to us in smallness, weakness, and hiddenness.

I find this a hopeful message. Somehow, I keep expecting loud and impressive events to convince me and others of God's saving power; but over and over again, I am reminded that spectacles, power plays, and big events are the ways of the world. Our temptation is to be distracted by them and made blind to the "shoot that shall sprout from the stump."

When I have no eyes for the small signs of God's presence—the smile of a baby, the carefree play of children, the words of encouragement and gestures of love offered by friends—I will always remain tempted to despair.

The small child of Bethlehem, the unknown young man of Nazareth, the rejected preacher, the naked man on the cross, he asks for my full attention. The work of our salvation takes place in the midst of a world that continues to shout, scream, and overwhelm us with its claims and promises. But the promise is hidden in the shoot that sprouts from the stump, a shoot that hardly anyone notices.

I remember seeing a film on the human misery and devastation brought by the bomb on Hiroshima. Among all the scenes of terror and despair, emerged one image of a man quietly writing a word in calligraphy. All his attention was directed to writing that one word. That image made this gruesome film a hopeful film. Isn't that what God is doing? Writing his Word in the midst of our dark world?

*Saints for the Season*

---

*DECEMBER 8: THE IMMACULATE CONCEPTION OF THE BLESSED VIRGIN MARY* celebrates the belief that Mary was conceived without any trace of Original Sin. In view of her role in our Salvation as the mother of Jesus, we celebrate the victory of God's grace, freely given to Mary. Pray with Mary for all couples who are struggling to conceive a child.

# Wait: Listen to Advent's Lesson

*Joan Chittister*

This Advent, when things seem bleaker than usual on every front, perhaps we must try to pray with a blank mind. Just wait. Don't focus on anything in particular. Don't want a single, specific thing. Then see what comes. And accept it, knowing that whatever it is it probably will not look like anything you were hoping to get. The baby did not look like God. The manger did not look like the kingdom. The place did not look promising. But in those things lay our salvation.

This Advent, just learn to wait. It's one of life's greatest lessons.

The ancients tell the story of a greathearted soul who ran through the streets of the city crying, "Power, greed and corruption. Power, greed and corruption."

For a time, at least, the attention of the people seemed to be riveted on this single-minded, openhearted person for whom all of life had become focused in one great question.

But then everyone went back to work, only slightly hearing, some downright annoyed.

Still, however, the cries continued.

Finally, one day, a child stepped in front of the wailing figure on a cold and stony night.

"Elder," the child said, "don't you realize that no one is listening to you?"

"Oh, of course I do, my child," the elder answered.

"Then why do you shout?" the child insisted, incredulous. "If nothing is changing, your efforts are useless."

"Oh no, dear child, these efforts are never useless," the elder said. "You see, I do not shout simply to change them. I shout so they cannot change me."

That is the fruit of Advent. That is the secret of waiting.

It is ourselves we must teach to listen. It is we who must wait again for new life, like all of those before us who waited for the "fullness of time."

 *Saints for the Season*

*DECEMBER 12: OUR LADY OF GUADALUPE,* the appearance of Mary to Juan Diego, is celebrated as a most joyous feast, particularly in the Hispanic culture. This day in 1531 marks the birth of a new people and a new inclusivity for the Catholic Church. Today reflect upon how your parish and neighborhood include people of different cultures and resolve to take some action to be more inclusive.

# $\mathcal{A}$DVENT, THE MOST DIFFICULT SEASON
### *Doris Donnelly*

$\mathcal{A}$dvent invites us to relive a pregnancy from the first moment of conception, when a seed was planted and took grip in the womb of a young woman who consented, freely, to become the mother of God. And we wait along with her to come to term. We watch with her and her husband—her not-to-be-forgotten husband—as they dream their dreams and express their fears for their unborn child.

We wait and watch with Mary, first of all, but just when we settle into thinking that Advent is about Mary and Joseph and the unborn Jesus, we catch sight of the other truth about Advent. That truth is that we, like Mary, are saluted and asked to bring forth a savior to a weary and hurting world. The Advent message is that the church—the mystical body of Christ—is pregnant with hope, filled with the Holy Spirit and that each one of us has been heralded, as Mary was, to be a Christbearer to a world desperately in need of all the saving it can get. It is a world that asks us to be eager and decisive in saying yes, so that newness will be given without delay.

---

*Think about these questions during the week. Feel free to write down your feelings and responses to the challenge of Advent in your personal journal:*

1.  How is your faith journey like a pregnancy?

2.  What does the world desperately need from you?

3.  How will you bear Christ into this world?

 *Saints for the Season*

*DECEMBER 13: SAINT LUCY* (d. 304) was a virgin who was martyred for her faith during the terrible reign of Emperor Diocletian. Patroness of Sicily and those suffering with eye disorders, Lucy is often pictured with two eyeballs on a plate. On a more joyful note, the Feast of Saint Lucy is celebrated among Europeans with a festival of lights. Celebrate today by lighting a candle in her honor and extending hospitality to a friend in darkness.

# The Season
of Christmas

# Christmas

Hot cider, cookies,
twinkling tree,
festive in its gilded ornamentation—
the smells and sights of the Christmas season.
In the north there is the expectation
of at least a dusting of snow.
The festivities last
longer than one day.
Ring in the New Year,
Epiphany,
Holy Family,
Solemnity of Mary,
the days of celebrating continue to brighten the January bleakness.
What is it we celebrate?
God the Father loved the world so much
that God sent the Son, the Word.
This Word of God, who called forth
something from nothing—the universe—
confined himself in human flesh to die on the Cross.
What kind of love is this?
The folly of the manger is the Cross.
One cannot gaze at the peasant couple
and shepherds grouped about the babe,
without the nagging reminder of what comes later.
Do we really dare welcome this kind of God
into our hearts at Christmas?
God's strange way of love
is found in the simple message
of the crib and Cross—
power is at its best in weakness.

*For love to yield its fullest force for good,*
*it appears, in human terms, to be weakness.*
*As we journey through the dark, winter days*
*of this holy, festive season,*
*let us learn to unleash our own power to love*
*in the weakness and pain,*
*in the brokenness and folly of our own lives.*

Carol A. Gura

---

*Be aware of the paradoxes of this season—the crib and*
*the Cross. Don't be surprised at the dark and pain-*
*ful aspects of this holiday amidst the glitter and joy.*
*Embrace it all!*

---

 Saints for the Season

DECEMBER 26: SAINT STEPHEN (d. ca. 35) was the first Christian martyr, stoned to death for his faith as recorded in the Acts of the Apostles. Chosen by the Twelve Apostles to be a leader (deacon) among the Hellenistic Christians, Stephen urged a more expansive approach to the mission of the early Church in preaching the Good News to the Gentiles. On this feast day think about your own openness to those who are different.

# Sharon's Christmas Prayer

*John Shea*

She was five,
sure of the facts,
and recited them
with slow solemnity,
convinced every word
was revelation.
She said
they were so poor
they had only peanut butter and jelly sandwiches
to eat
and they went a long way from home
without getting lost. The lady rode
a donkey, the man walked, and the baby
was inside the lady.

They had to stay in a stable
with an ox and an ass (hee-hee)
but the Three Rich Men found them
because a star lited the roof.
Shepherds came and you could
pet the sheep but not feed them.
Then the baby was borned.
And do you know who he was?
    Her quarter eyes inflated
    to silver dollars.
The baby was God.
    And she jumped in the air,
    whirled round, dove into the sofa,
    and buried her head under the cushion
    which is the only proper response
    to the Good News of the Incarnation.

---

*Enter this Christmas Day with the eyes of a child. In the evening write down what you observed today, from this childlike perspective. How will you celebrate the fact that "this baby was God"?*

 *Saints for the Season*

DECEMBER 27: SAINT JOHN, APOSTLE AND EVANGELIST, with his brothers James and Peter, was one of the closest followers of Jesus from among the Twelve. Traditionally attributed as the writer of the Fourth Gospel, John, a leader of the first Christians in Jerusalem, accompanied Peter to preach the Gospel in Samaria and later established a community at Ephesus. Read the first chapter of John's Gospel as a meditation for today.

# THE WISE MAN

*Clarissa Pinkola Estés*

The beloved Bal Shem Tov was dying and sent for his disciples. "I have acted as intermediary for you, and now when I am gone you must do this for yourselves. You know the place in the forest where I call to God? Stand there in that place and do the same. You know how to light the fire, and how to say the prayer. Do all of these and God will come."

After the Bal Shem Tov died, the first generation did exactly as he had instructed, and God always came. But by the second generation, the people had forgotten how to light the fire in the way the Bal Shem Tov had taught them. Nevertheless, they stood in the special place in the forest and they said the prayer, and God came.

By the third generation, the people had forgotten how to light the fire, and they had forgotten the place in the forest. But they spoke the prayer nevertheless, and God still came.

In the fourth generation, everyone had forgotten how to build the fire, and no one any longer knew just where in the forest one should stand, and finally, too, the prayer itself could not be recalled. But one person still remembered the story about it all, and told it aloud. And God still came.

*The Gift of Story* by Clarissa Pinkola Estés, Ph.D.,
Copyright © 1993. All rights reserved.

---

*This, then, is the power of the story. What does this teach about the importance of the Christmas story? Write some of your ideas in your personal journal. Spend some time thinking about this little story. Let it bring to mind some of the stories of your own family. Write one of these stories. During the holidays, tell the story when the extended family is gathered, and ask others to share their stories.*

## Saints for the Season

*DECEMBER 29: SAINT THOMAS BECKET* (ca. 1118–1170) was the archbishop of Canterbury who was martyred for his stand against King Henry II of England. After a conversion experience, Thomas resigned his post as chancellor, adopted an austere lifestyle, and was in open conflict with the king over secular and spiritual jurisdictions. Think about those situations in your life where you need to take a stand against injustice.

# REALIZATION

### Thomas Merton

In Louisville, at the corner of Fourth and Walnut, in the center of the shopping district, I was suddenly overwhelmed with the realization that I loved all those people, that they were mine and I theirs, that we could not be alien to one another even though we were total strangers. It was like waking from a dream of separateness, of spurious self-isolation in a special world, the world of renunciation and supposed holiness. The whole illusion of a separate holy existence is a dream. Not that I question the reality of my vocation, or of my monastic life: but the conception of "separation from the world" that we have in the monastery too easily presents itself as a complete illusion: the illusion that by making vows we become a different species of being, pseudoangels, "spiritual men," men of interior life, what have you.

Certainly these traditional values are very real, but their reality is not of an order outside everyday existence in a contingent world, nor does it entitle one to despise the secular: though "out of the world" we are in the same world as everybody else, the world of the bomb, the world of race hatred, the world of technology, the world of mass media, big business, revolution, and all the rest. We take a different attitude to all these things, for we belong to God. Yet so does everybody else belong to God. We just happen to be conscious of it, and to make a profession out of this consciousness. But does that entitle us to consider ourselves different, or even better, than others? The whole idea is preposterous.

This sense of liberation from an illusory difference was such a relief and such a joy to me that I almost laughed out loud. And I suppose my happiness could have taken form in the words: "Thank God, thank God that I am like other men, that I am only a man among others." To think that for sixteen or seventeen years I have been taking seriously this pure illusion that is implicit in so much of our monastic thinking.

It is a glorious destiny to be a member of the human race, though it is a race dedicated to many absurdities and one which makes many terrible mistakes: yet, with all that, God Himself gloried in becoming a member of the human race. A member of the human race! To think that such a commonplace realization should suddenly seem like news that one holds the winning ticket in a cosmic sweepstake.

I have the immense joy of being man, a member of a race in which God Himself became incarnate. As if the sorrows and stupidities of the human condition could over-whelm me, now I realize what we all are. And if only everybody could realize this! But it cannot be explained. There is no way of telling people that they are all walking around shining like the sun.

*Saints for the Season*

*JANUARY 2: SAINTS BASIL THE GREAT AND GREGORY NAZIANZEN* are two great fourth-century theologians whose troubled friendship shaped both their lives. Basil, bishop of Caesarea, brought the Arian controversy to a close (Arianism denied the divinity of Christ and the Holy Spirit). He is noted for his relief efforts during a famine in Cappadocia and was named a Doctor of the Church because of his theological works. Gregory was affected by the conflict with Basil at the Council of Constantinople and retreated to Nazianzus to write theological orations, poetry, and numerous letters. Gregory is noted for his clarity on the Trinity and the procession of the Holy Spirit. Today you might choose to write your beliefs about God the Father, Jesus the Son, and the Holy Spirit the Sanctifier.

# WATER AND THE SPIRIT
### Elizabeth A. Johnson

Water is elemental, absolutely essential for life as we know it, although like fire it too can kill. On this planet life began in the primeval seas, and human and other mammalian life continues to originate in the water of the womb. Sap in the tree, dew on the grass, blood in the veins, wine in the vessel, rain on the earth, water outpoured: all bespeak the active presence of God. As a symbol of the Spirit, water points to the bottomless wellspring of the source of life and to the refreshment and gladness that result from deep immersion in this mystery.

Scripture is replete with instances where water symbolizes the Spirit of life. Speaking through the prophet Ezekiel, God promises that the people will find their true heart: "I will sprinkle clean water upon you . . . and a new spirit I will put within you; and I will remove from your body the heart of stone and give you a heart of flesh" (Ez 36:25–26). In Isaiah's vision, justice and peace in the human world and the natural world are the gifts that result when the Spirit, like a cascade of water from a vessel, is poured out (Is 32:15–18). For Joel, sons and daughters will prophesy and even the old will dream again when drenched with this Spirit poured out on all flesh (Jl 2:28–29). This same Spirit is the living water Jesus promised to the Samaritan woman, a spring of love welling up at the core of creation (Jn 4:7–15). As Paul points out to the Romans, God overflows in the depth of the divine being and from there "the love of God is poured into our hearts by the Holy Spirit given to us" (Rom 5:5).

---

*As you think about the baptism of Jesus this week, take time each day to look up the passages noted on the previous page and meditate upon their meaning for you. Reflect upon the images of water that are mentioned as you come to more fully understand the power of the Holy Spirit in your own life. Compose your own prayer to the Holy Spirit, using these images and other insights into the power of the Spirit, who comes to us in Baptism.*

 *Saints for the Season*

JANUARY 4: SAINT ELIZABETH ANN SETON (1774–1821) is the first American-born Saint. Widowed during a trip to Italy with her husband and children, Elizabeth Ann Bayley Seton converted to Catholicism because of the kindness of an Italian family. She is noted for opening a school for girls, opening a school for the poor children of Emmitsburg, and founding the Sisters of Charity. Take time today to reflect upon your own conversion and ask God to show you what work of love you are called to inaugurate.

# The Season
## of Lent

# Lent

Under the blanket of snow
shades of brown, scrubby,
matted grass peaks through
in the colder North.
The bleakness even covers the rainy winter season
of Southern and Western climates.
All lies dormant, dreary, and dark.
All is resting for a time—
time to recoup, refresh, to reenergize.
This is nature's way of preparing for the first bursts of spring.
This gloomy season of winter holds within
its embrace the Lenten bleakness of
the parade of Christians, each waiting
to be marked with the ashen cross.
Reminder of deaths: winters, loved ones, our own—
let us pray for the courage to mourn them all.

Eager to jump quickly into spring,
the longer but colder days hem us in.
Eager to leap into Easter's alleluias,
Lent draws us back
inward to face the cross.

We need winter's solace and Lent's sacrifice
to bring us round,
cleaned and scrubbed;
fasted and forgiven,
prayed and reflected;
given and giving up.

*In secret we know how much we need*
*these forty days.*
*Facing the cross brings us to that place where*
*we can truly know the glories of Easter—*
*sending up its tender green shoots*
*of gratitude,*
*grace,*
*and wisdom.*

Carol A. Gura

---

*During this Lenten season take up the age-old traditions*
*of prayer, fasting, and almsgiving. Decide how you will*
*nurture your soul with extended time for prayer; empty*
*your cluttered life through fasting; and embrace the poor*
*and needy by giving of your time, talent, and treasure.*

---

 *Saints for the Season*

---

*MARCH 3: SAINT KATHARINE DREXEL* (1858–1955) was a Philadelphia-born heiress who devoted her life and fortune to serving the black and Native Americans. She founded the Sisters of the Blessed Sacrament, who are dedicated to the education of African and Native Americans. In 1925 she founded the first Catholic university designed for African Americans—Xavier University, in New Orleans. Reflect upon your openness to people of the African and Native American cultures. Pray for forgiveness for the atrocities these people have suffered.

# Seasons of Personal Examination
### Elizabeth J. Canham

When we are drawn by God into seasons of personal examination and penitence, we are aided by the Spirit who guides us into all truth (John 16:13). To set out on a self-directed, critical evaluation that is not marinated in the grace of the Gospel is to court hopelessness and depression. So we begin our residence in the divine clutch clinic prayerfully, asking the Spirit to guide us, and our first act of letting go is the acknowledgment that we cannot manage alone. In the context of a culture that encourages independence and autonomy, the desire to control all too easily dictates our actions, even our prayer. Asking for help is a first step toward humility and conversion. It is a handing over of the unconscious arrogance that assumes if we work hard enough we can become who we are meant to be. By this willingness to let go we come to know with the mind of Christ, and learn to walk with him into the recesses of heart and mind to clear out the clutter. And this is where the struggle begins, for we find ourselves attached to what we have, and fearful of the changes we perceive as diminishment.

At the beginning of his ministry, Jesus retired to the barren hills of Judea for a period of reflection and preparation. In Mark's version of the temptation narrative, Jesus is driven by the Spirit into the wilderness, a strong declaration of being sent out or expelled that seems to suggest a divine necessity. In the time of testing that followed, Jesus was presented with choices that would either set him free to fulfill God's call, or encumber him with a self-image dependent on the affirmation and deference of others. The clutch clinic of the Judean desert compelled Jesus to relinquish the way of instant gratification, alignment with sociopolitical power structures, and self-aggrandizement. He returned to Galilee with open hands, ready to risk himself for God and proclaim the Gospel of repentance and forgiveness.

The sense of being driven, compelled by the Spirit to remain in the place where my clutching would be challenged, generated a lot of resistance, yet in the struggles with self-will there continued to be an undergirding grace enabling me to uncurl tight fingers.

_____

*Ask the Holy Spirit to be with you as you embark on this Lenten time of penance and conversion. How does it feel to let go and let God? Reflect upon the clutter that fills your days and your heart. Practice letting go of this clutter, one day at a time. Make a list of the clutter you wish to clear out:*

1. What things, people, or ideas do you sense have a great hold on you?
2. What do you continue to clutch?

*Pray for the grace of letting go. Journal your experience of
letting go in order to meet this time of Lent with open hands.*

 *Saints for the Season*

MARCH 7: SAINTS PERPETUA AND FELICITY (d. 203) were both nursing
mothers, separated from their infants for the love of Christ, who were martyred under
the persecution of Diocletian. Perpetua was a visionary who consistently manifested
the presence of the Holy Spirit. Felicity was the servant of Perpetua. Pray today for all
infants who have been abused and abandoned by their mothers.

# THOU ART DUST
## Joseph McLellan

The fact that we are dust is a basic fact of human life. Not the only fact, for we
are dust that acts and thinks and feels within it the stirrings of eternity. But dust—
limitation, imperfection and a due measure of unhappiness—is the condition of every
man [and woman], and if we do not remind ourselves of it we will surely be reminded
by what happens in our daily lives. So it is good to have the gentle reminder of Ash
Wednesday to focus our awareness on our limitations.

But Ash Wednesday is not a feast of despair; it is a feast of humility. If we are indeed
dust, we are dust that has been raised by God to a higher status, dust that aspires to union
with God. The message of Lent—suffering and confrontation with the facts of sin and
death—leads naturally into the message of Easter—joy and resurrection. The two are
linked inseparably; without Easter ahead, Ash Wednesday and Lent would be worse than
meaningless: morbid. But without Ash Wednesday and the forty special days that follow
it, there would be no need for Easter, no significance to it.

The relation is not merely one of contrast. Lent and Easter are a single reality, existing forever together although we live them one at a time. Without both, our view of the human condition is incomplete. And so, as we kneel on Ash Wednesday and take upon our foreheads the reminder of our mortality, we should look ahead at the same time to Easter and the promise of immortality.

 *Saints for the Season*

*MARCH 8: SAINT JOHN OF GOD* (1495–1550) is the patron of the sick and of hospitals. John's moving conversion upon hearing a sermon of Saint John of Ávila caused him to found a religious community devoted to the care of the sick and the poor. Today visit someone who is sick, whether homebound or in the hospital. Find out what your parish does to care for the sick and get involved.

# THE GALE WINDS OF MARCH
*Ken Gire*

The soul is like a bird,
shaken from its peaceful roost by the inclement
    circumstances of life,
where windblown branches
and sudden gusts from darkening horizons
thrust it into weather that is wild and uncertain.
And sometimes, however hard we beat our wings,
we can't seem to overcome the elements galing against us.
We are thrashed about in the air,
windsheered and weary,
wondering if our cries for help are reaching God.

But then the tempest subsides,
for a while anyway,
and the updrafts of God's Spirit lift us to new heights,
above the winds, above the rain, above the earth.
And, for a moment,
we soar.

---

*Pray this meditation several times this week, thinking about your own life. You may wish to write some of your own thoughts in your journal. These questions will guide your prayer time:*

1. Which images in the prayer-poem describe your life experience?

2. As you journey toward initiation, how has your soul experienced the "updrafts of God's Spirit"?

3. How else is your soul like a bird?

 *Saints for the Season*

MARCH 9: SAINT FRANCES OF ROME (1384–1440) founded a community of women to care for the poor while her husband was still living. Happily married for forty years, she is a model for housewives. After her husband's death, Frances joined the community and became its superior. She is the patron of motorists. Pray today for those who make their living by driving.

# PRAYER IS LETTING GOD LOVE US

*L. Patrick Carroll*

When we ask ourselves why we pray we may get a variety of answers. Sometimes we speak as though we pray to get God to "shape up." We ask God repeatedly to take care of something that God apparently does not want to deal with, on the outside chance that if we ask often and loudly enough God's mind will change. "Oh, God," we pray, "bring peace to our world," or "help my uncle Jack," or "end world hunger," or "let me stop drinking." All of those are good things to pray for, but, unreflectively, we may be asking God to do something so that we don't have to. Our prayers of petition at eucharist often sound like we are cajoling God rather that committing ourselves. I believe that underneath all of our prayers must be the hope that we, rather than God, will be transformed so that, with God, we can do our part to bring whatever we pray for to be.

Rather than an unarguable, theological answer to the question, "Why do we pray?" I give only my answer. I pray because I need to let God love me. Prayer, for me, is essentially that. I pray because I am so inclined to forget that I am God's beloved son. I forget that I am not alone in the struggles of my life. I forget that the waters will overwhelm me unless I keep my eyes on the one who is calling me to himself across the waves. I pray because I need regularly to remember God's love. I read scripture to help me remember. I celebrate eucharist because it reminds me of God's love for me, for us, in Jesus, though I am part of a stumbling, unfaithful people. Over and over, I come together with a community so that God can love us to life, create clean hearts in us, make us into the body that we say we are. I pray individually and with communities so that I can see the face of Christ shining in me, on me and around me.

 *Saints for the Season*

*MARCH 17: SAINT PATRICK* (ca. 390–461) is well known as the apostle to Ireland. Born in Britain, he was the son of a deacon and grandson of a priest. Captured by border raiders, Patrick spent some years as a slave in Ireland. Upon his return to Britain, he was ordained a priest and devoted his life to evangelizing Ireland. Patrick preached against slavery. Reflect upon the effects of slavery in the United States and other parts of the world. Resolve to take an action in imitation of Patrick.

# My Help Is in the Mountain
### Nancy Wood

My help is in the mountain
Where I take myself to heal
The earthly wounds
That people give to me.
I find a rock with sun on it
And a stream where the water runs gentle
And the trees which one by one give me company.
So must I stay for a long time
Until I have grown from the rock
And the stream is running through me
And I cannot tell myself from one tall tree.
Then I know that nothing touches me
Nor makes me run away.
My help is in the mountain
That I take away with me.

*Take a walk outdoors sometime this week. Enjoy the created world and think about where you find help. When you return, reread the poem and respond by writing your own thoughts. These questions may be helpful:*

1. How does the poet find solace in nature?

2. What does it mean to become "grown from the rock"?

3. What is your own experience of the "stream running through you"?

*As you continue this Lenten journey and your own process of initiation, allow God's created world to speak to your own need for healing.*

 *Saints for the Season*

MARCH 19: SAINT JOSEPH, husband of Mary and father of Jesus, holds a special place in the history of our Salvation. All we know of Joseph from the Scriptures is that he was obedient to the messages of God sent to him in dreams and that he was a carpenter by trade. Joseph is honored as patron of Italians, who celebrate his feast with festive meals. A plate, heaped high with food, is set for Saint Joseph and later given to the poor. Joseph is also the patron of those seeking a spouse. Today invite someone to dinner and celebrate this day honoring Saint Joseph.

# AFTERMATH

*Carol A. Gura*

Somehow I keep putting my foot into my mouth. Now I have really done it. He said, "Before the cock crows, you will deny me three times." How could I be so weak when I was chosen to lead? How could I run away from someone I love so much? What is wrong with me?

As I sit in the middle of this thunderstorm on the top of the very hill where he was crucified—Golgotha—my mind goes back to all the times I messed up. There was the time a great storm blew up on the lake. So brave was I that I reassured all the other followers and even walked on water. But my eternal flaw, I looked down at the swirling water and sank. Me, the fearless one, soaking wet as the Master admonished me, "O you of little faith." Then there was the time I tried to play God. Oh, yes, I tried to tell him not to go to Jerusalem to die. He swore at me, "Get behind me, Satan." How could I be so stupid? Even after he picked me out of the twelve, me and James and John. We were special enough to go up to the top of Mount Tabor and see the Lord transfigured before our very eyes. I was so ecstatic that I wanted to build three tents and stay there forever. How naive of me. But this tops all my blunders. As the thunder cracks around me and the night draws into deep black, my heart is broken. I am so ashamed. Now he is dead and I denied him, just as he had foretold.

I am smeared with mud from rending my clothes and groveling on the ground. In my desolation I cry out to God. In my despair the words of David are on my lips: "To you, O LORD, I call; my rock, do not refuse to hear me, for if you are silent to me, I shall be like those who go down to the Pit. Hear the voice of my supplication, as I cry to you for help, as I lift up my hands toward your most holy sanctuary. Do not drag me away with the wicked, with those who are workers of evil, who speak peace with their neighbors, while mischief is in their hearts" (Psalm 28:1–3). From the depths of my prayer, I emerge. The rain has slowed to a patter and the night crickets begin their song. It is like a hymn of praise to God. I can only utter my gratitude, "Blessed be the LORD, for he has heard the sound of my pleadings. The LORD is my strength and my shield; in him my heart trusts; so I am helped, and my heart exults, and with my song I give thanks to him" (Psalm 28:6–7).

*Join Peter on the hill after Jesus' Death. As you meditate with Peter on your own weakness, think about how often you have found God to be your strength. Recall the unconditional acceptance and forgiveness God has offered to you. Write your own meditation by naming your sinfulness and the ways God has forgiven you.*

 *Saints for the Season*

*MARCH 25: THE ANNUNCIATION OF THE LORD.* Today the Church celebrates the announcement that Mary would be the Mother of the Messiah. The Angel Gabriel speaks to her of this strange and unusual pregnancy. Mary's simple "yes" is a model for all believers who are challenged by God's plan for their life. Pray the *Magnificat* found in Luke 1:46–55, and be open to God's blessings in your life.

# The Season of Easter

# Easter

Spring, the harbinger of rich harvests
and rainbow-colored flowers,
comes in rain and wind and sun.
A long walk amidst earth, ripe and rich in her dark scent,
yields a vision of purple, gold, and white crocus,
clumped next to rock and rotting trees;
daffodils peeking up out of her rich brown soil
nod their "Amen" in the balmy breeze.
Welcome to the sun, whose brilliance blinds us
in the light of Christ.
Welcome the Easter candle and fire that burnishes us
with cleansing power.
Welcome the waters of baptismal sprinkling and dousing,
through living water we pass from death to new life.
The Easter promise, like that of spring:
All that is dead will live again,
alive in Christ who died and rose to give us life!
Alleluia! Alleluia! Alleluia!
What was shattered will be made whole,
the original blessing of unity is, once again,
restored through the power of the Resurrection!
Alleluia! Alleluia! Alleluia!
All evil is overpowered, washed clean, forgiven.
We need not fear or fret or despair,
the Blood of the Lamb has saved us!
Alleluia! Alleluia! Alleluia!

Carol A. Gura

*Easter is a time of blessing, an attitude of gratitude toward all of life. It is in times like this that we need to hold on to the bright promises of Easter. As you journey through the Easter season, allow these pages and the scriptures for the Sunday liturgies to speak their bright promise to your heart.*

 *Saints for the Season*

*APRIL 21: SAINT ANSELM* (1033–1109) was a prolific writer of letters, prayers, and theological treatises. His later work includes a definition of free will and its compatibility with divine grace. He characterized his theological works as "faith seeking understanding." Be mindful of the faith that has brought you to this moment in your journey of conversion. Today pray for an increase of the gift of faith.

# HE IS RISEN
## Thomas Merton

So we are called not only to believe that Christ once rose from the dead, thereby proving that he was God; we are called to experience the Resurrection in our own lives by entering into this dynamic movement, by following Christ who lives in us. This life, this dynamism, is expressed by the power of love and of encounter: Christ lives in us if we love one another. And our love for one another means involvement in one another's history. Christ lives in us and leads us, through mutual encounter and commitment, into a new future which we build together for one another. That future is called the Kingdom of God. The Kingdom is already established; the Kingdom is a present reality. But there is still work to be done. Christ calls us to work together in building his Kingdom. We cooperate with him in bringing it to perfection. Such is the timeless message of the Church not only on Easter Sunday but on every day of the year and every year until the world's end. The dynamism of the Easter mystery is at the heart of the Christian faith. It is the life of the Church. The Resurrection is not a doctrine we try to prove or a problem we argue about; it is the life and action of Christ himself in us by his Holy Spirit.

 *Saints for the Season*

*APRIL 28: SAINT PETER CHANEL* (1803–1841) was born, reared, and ordained a Marist priest in France. He was sent to Oceania as a missionary where a tribal chief, learning his own son was to be baptized, had Peter murdered. But, even though the chief silenced Peter, the whole island where he preached converted to Christianity within two years. Reflect upon your own Baptism or desire to be baptized today. Why is Baptism important to you?

## GRACE
*Wendell Berry*

The woods is shining this morning;
red, gold and green, the leaves
lie on the ground, or fall,
or hang full of light in the air still.
Perfect in its rise and in its fall, it takes
the place it has been coming to forever.
It has not hastened here, or lagged.
See how surely it has sought itself,
its roots passing lordly through the earth.

See how without confusion it is
all that is, and how flawless
its grace is. Running or walking the way
is the same. Be still. Be still.
"He moves your bones, and the way is clear."

 *Saints for the Season*

*APRIL 29: SAINT CATHERINE OF SIENA* (1347–1380) was born in Siena, Italy, and experienced her first mystical vision at the age of seven. As a Dominican, Catherine worked with the sick and accompanied those on death row to the gallows. Her writings and holiness were so evident that she was advisor to Popes and was named a Doctor of the Church. Today pray for those on death row and think about your stand on capital punishment.

# THE ROAD OF TRUST

*Macrina Wiederkehr*

The road to Emmaus is not a road of the past.
It is an everyday road
Someone is still walking along beside us
    explaining the scriptures to us
    breaking bread with us.
    and then vanishing from our sight.

And we are still rather slow
    about recognizing what's happening
    in the breaking of the bread,
    and that's because
    we are slow about trusting.

It takes so long to be a Church.
We seem unable
    to trust the struggle as divine
    and even in the struggle
    to cry out:
    It is the Lord!

We long to recognize Christ
    before we trust
    the stranger he sends down our road,
And so
    often
    we miss the blessing.

It is not that
    we're on the wrong road.
It is rather
    that we fail
    to trust
    and recognize
    strangers.
The road
    we walk each day
    is
    the road to Emmaus.

*You may wish to read Luke 24:13–35, along with the prayer-poem on the journey to Emmaus. Then ask yourself:*

1. When have I recognized Christ in a stranger recently?

2. What can I do to begin to trust the strangers I meet?

3. How can I grasp the full implications of the daily journey to Emmaus suggested in the prayer?

*In your journal write down your understanding of the "breaking of the bread," explaining why trust is needed.*

 *Saints for the Season*

MAY 1: *SAINT JOSEPH THE WORKER* is celebrated today. This is a day to celebrate and give thanks for all those who work, especially at various trades. Joseph is said to have been a carpenter. Take time today to make "put-off" repairs around the house.

# THE PATTERN

*John Moffit*

"Why are you disturbed? Why do these doubts
Rise in your hearts? See my hands and my feet,
That it is I myself. Feel me and see."

Faced with this huge hint of resurrection
Mankind labors, doubting how to take it;
Waits as on that first day of the week,
Yearning to believe and yet not ready
To grasp the plausible showings now momently
Opened on all sides . . .

matter caught up
Always into fresh forms, from atom to amoeba;
The watchful man; clean sunlight, textures, sounds
Translated through a miracle in the cells
To enterprise of art, of faith; the fathomless play
Of a cosmos seized in the microcosm of mind,
Raised to a person—being, knowing, loving—
True image of his source; mankind itself
Offered at last in a total holocaust,
Lifting with itself a whole creation;
No single soul against its will left out,
Not one iota of all space and time
But offered some share in the continuing rite,
Which ceases at time's end . . .

but still, like those
Disciples, believing what's been shown to them,
taggered by the sheer ubiquity of it.
"Have you anything to eat?" he said. They gave him
A piece of broiled fish and a honeycomb.
And he, after he had eaten there before them,
Took what was left and made them also eat.

## Saints for the Season

*MAY 14: SAINT MATTHIAS* was the Apostle chosen to replace Judas. Little is known of his work, but legend has it that Matthias preached to cannibals, was taken prisoner, and later was rescued by Andrew the Apostle. Develop the practice of prayer when making important decisions.

# *S*PRING SONG
### Lucille Clifton

*t*he green of Jesus
is breaking the ground
and the sweet
smell of delicious Jesus
is opening the house and
the dance of Jesus music
has hold of the air and
the world is turning
in the body of Jesus and
the future is possible

---

*Think about these images of Jesus: the green of Jesus, the smell of Jesus, the dance of Jesus, and the body of Jesus. How does Jesus—fully human and fully divine—make your future possible? Journal your insights in the space provided. Recall a time when you have felt as the poet did. Write that experience of Jesus during this next week.*

*Saints for the Season*

*MAY 25: SAINT MARY MAGDALENE DE' PAZZI* (1566–1607), a mystic, was a Carmelite nun in Italy. This Saint whose feast is celebrated today calls us to take inventory of our own spiritual life. Begin this day in prayer and seek God's guidance as you follow your journey of faith.

## SPRING
### Annie Dillard

Like many of us, spring brings with it reminders of much to do and the excitement of cleaning off the grime of winter. Annie Dillard voices the feelings of many.

> It is spring. I plan to try to control myself this year, to watch the progress of the season in a calm and orderly fashion. In spring I am prone to wretched excess. I abandon myself to flights and compulsions; I veer into various states of physical disarray.

Name some of your own feelings, anxieties, or compulsions this spring.

Now read on to see how Annie fared with her resolve.

> The morning woods were utterly new. A strong yellow light pooled between the trees; my shadow appeared and vanished on the path, since a third of the trees I walked under were still bare, a third spread a luminous haze wherever they grew, and another third blocked the sun with new, whole leaves. The snakes were out—I saw a bright, smashed one on the path—and the butterflies were vaulting and furling about; the phlox was at its peak, and even the evergreens looked greener, newly created and washed.
>
> Long racemes of white flowers hung from the locust trees. Last summer I heard a Cherokee legend about the locust tree and the moon. The moon goddess starts out with a big ball, the full moon, and she hurls it across the sky. She spends all day retrieving it; then she shaves a slice from it and hurls it again, retrieving, shaving, hurling, and so on.

She uses up a moon a month, all year. Then, the way Park Service geologist Bill Wellman tells it, "long about spring of course she's knee-deep in moon-shavings," so she finds her favorite tree, the locust, and hangs the slender shavings from its boughs. And there they were, the locust flowers, pale and clustered in crescents.

*Take a walk this week and allow the peace of spring to enter your soul. Remember that Jesus left us his gift of peace. Sit on the grass or on a rock and meditate on the beauty of nature, allowing it to teach you about peace. Write about your experience, your meditation, and the peace you received. Know that you can come back to that peace just by going outdoors and beholding the wonder of God's presence.*

 *Saints for the Season*

*MAY 26: SAINT PHILIP NERI* (1515–1595) was noted for his prayer and generosity, particularly in his work with the sick and with pilgrims. He founded the Congregation of the Oratory, which promoted the holiness of priestly life and good preaching. Pray today for the priests who have touched your life.

# REMEMBERING

*Carol A. Gura*

Connected, we breathe the same air,
    share our pollutions.
We drink in beauty, all green,
    flowered in every color of the rainbow.

Waters from far-off oceans and rivers
    become our common cup—
        to quench our thirst for life, justice, peace.

That incredible blazing sun-star
    sets and rises,
        steadying us even in her departure
            through reflected moonlight.

We are all connected!
    Seasons—birth, life, harvest, death, decay—cycles
        are lived inescapably by us all,
            carried by our bodies' continual changing.

We carry in us the universe,
    linking us, one to each other,
        to each living thing,
            to each particle of creation.

Why do we think we are separate?
Why do we have such a hard time remembering?

---

*Think about all the ways you are connected to others and the entire created world. Write down some of these connections. Reflect upon all the ways we separate ourselves from one another. Meditate on Jesus' prayer of unity from John 17:20–26. Write your own thoughts as to how you can bring about that unity.*

 *Saints for the Season*

*MAY 27: SAINT AUGUSTINE OF CANTERBURY* (d. ca. 605) was the apostle to the English and the first archbishop of Canterbury. An Italian missionary, Augustine was sent with forty monks to England to convert the Anglo-Saxons. Today reflect upon the role of the baptized to evangelize. Take one action to proclaim the Good News among co-workers or friends today.

# PENTECOST

*Ann Johnson*

Here I am, Yahweh,
    afire with some unnamed energy.

Today was just a common day.
After early prayer and eating
    we met together in one room.
The quiet was so deep,
    my mind stilled,
    supported by the sturdiness of our silence.

Suddenly, we heard a rushing sound,
    as being born of a wind.
      Violent, it filled the house where we were sitting.
      There appeared to us scattered tongues of a fire,
      which alighted on each one of us.
In awe we watched,
    and now
Here I am, Yahweh,
    afire with some unnamed energy.

This moment was just a common moment.
I am often stilled and strengthened by our prayer.
The chanting fills my throat with resonant balm
    and my ears channel the ancient melodies
    to calm my stirring mind.
    Times of quiet breathing are a symphony.
    Words of sharing feed my soul.
We sit in bodily harmony
    and sense that we are more together than we are each alone.
    Today, in time-suspended sitting,
    like a seasoned log cast upon the reddened coals
    unwatched and dormant,
    I suddenly burst into flames.
Here I am, Yahweh,
    afire with some unnamed energy.

This time becomes the common time.
As I look up and dare to gaze at those here gathered,
    I see the spirit shared.
Each sister's eyes aglow with wondrous infusion
    and color high upon the bearded brothers' cheeks.

I see you, my companions!
I see you in all that it means to see.
    In that flaming recognition we ignite in sounds and syllables
    synonymous with utterings of devoted people everywhere,
    who, like ourselves,
    sing and sigh in consonance with God.

And I, so aging and respected,
I, so simple in my speech,
I, Miryam
    am in the midst of us as we spill out into the street.
    Speaking the tongues of many!
    Amazing and most wonderful!
    Chattering as though over-filled with sweet wine!
    A spirit effervescent, almost o'er done,
Until I cried, "Enough! Yahweh, enough!"

Here I am, Yahweh,
    afire with some unnamed energy.

This fiery fervor I bequeath to common people
    everywhere and for all time.
I give you sturdy, strengthening prayer together,
    supported and sustained by chanted rhythms and ancient
      sounds;
    deepened and united in harmonious breathing and shared
      stillness;
    exchanging words and gazes,
    open, faithful, undefended
    until like seasoned logs
    cast upon the reddened coals of your inheritance,
    unwatched and dormant,
    your spirits conflagrate.

I give you common songs to sing and dances,
    laughter, tears and kisses.

I give you people who will watch in wonder
    at the sight of the bonding of your spirits.
    Who will weep in loneliness as they witness the holy fire
    that welds you to each other.

I give you eternal words to open your gentle glowing hearts
    as you go out to meet the iron bands of fear and dogma.
Witness to the searching faithfully.
Warm the people. Pitch your tent in the midst of them.
Nurture the fire.
Make space in the prayer circle.
Embrace the lonely.
Incorporate the peaceful Way.
Journey in the deserts of your time.
Know yourself and your company of special people.
Lay your hands upon each other
    that each may know the resurrecting way,
    that each may cry in joy.
Here I am, Yahweh,
    afire with an unnamed energy.

 *Saints for the Season*

*MAY 30: SAINT JOAN OF ARC* (1412–1431) was burned at the stake for witchcraft, for she heard God's voice telling her to lead the French army against the English. Today remember all those women who were burned or executed as witches for following the inner voice of God.

# Ordinary Time

# Ordinary Time

Daylilies bob their heads in the soft breezes of summer,
   short-lived blossoms, day-long showy yellow,
      orange, mauve, and rust.
   Tomorrow new blooms will take their place
      in vibrant rich colors.
The long-awaited brilliance of the sun,
      through the dreary days of winter
      and showers of spring's pale green openings,
      through it all we long for summer's heat;
      summer's lush, rich colors;
      summer's lightning zags tearing through
         the late afternoon sky.
Long awaited too is ordinary time—those lazy summer days,
      marking our days,
      readying us to greet fall's harvest.
Plain, ordinary time—
      no fasting or feasting, just common simple time;
      days drifting into nights, then dawning
         into new days again.
Time for mowing the lawn, playing with babies,
         baseball, and tennis;
      plenty of time for picnics, fixing up, and making new.

Ordinary time is God's time—time for extraordinary miracles;
      time for changing
         water into wine, seeds into flowers—
         plants yielding ripe, red tomatoes;

*trees bending boughs, heavy with apples and pears;*
*time for changing*
*tears into laughter, into hugs,*
*into full-blown kisses on the mouth,*
*losses into wisdom, into gratitude,*
*into the fullness of richly blessed lives.*
*Our lives are as short-lived as the lily of the day.*
*We nod with the gentle breezes of God's Spirit.*
*The rich and varied hues of our colors*
*are painted by the brush of the Artist,*
*who takes the ordinary, commonplace times of our lives*
*and adorns the universe with our presence.*
*Let us take notice of Your ways of keeping ordinary times.*
*Let us keep time with You.*

Carol A. Gura

---

*During Ordinary Time, discover the ways God works in extraordinary ways in your life. Ordinary Time calls us to be vigilant and keenly aware of the simple and common things of life.*

---

 ## Saints for the Season

JANUARY 24: SAINT FRANCIS DE SALES (1567–1622), the bishop of Geneva, is known for the spiritual direction he offered to clergy and laity. His writings, sermons, and letters made the spiritual tradition of the Church relevant for the people. To celebrate the feast of this Doctor of the Church, read from a spiritual book today or share a conversation with a spiritual companion.

# *T*HE WINGÈD LIFE

*Anne Morrow Lindbergh*

*A* good relationship has a pattern like a dance and is built on some of the same rules. The partners do not need to hold on tightly, because they move confidently in the same pattern, intricate but gay and swift and free, like a country dance of Mozart's. To touch heavily would be to arrest the pattern and freeze the movement, to check the endlessly changing beauty of its unfolding. There is no place here for the possessive clutch, the clinging arm, the heavy hand; only the barest touch in passing. Now arm in arm, now face to face, now back to back—it does not matter which. Because they know they are partners moving to the same rhythm, creating a pattern together, and being invisibly nourished by it.

The joy of such a pattern is not only the joy of creation or the joy of participation, it is also the joy of living in the moment. Lightness of touch and living in the moment are intertwined. One cannot dance well unless one is completely in time with the music, not leaning back to the last step or pressing forward to the next one, but poised directly on the present step as it comes. Perfect poise on the beat is what gives good dancing its sense of ease, of timelessness, of the eternal. . . . The dancers who are perfectly in time never destroy "the wingèd life" in each other or in themselves.

*As you read the passage from* Gift from the Sea *on the previous page, think about your most intimate relationships—marriage partner, best friends, a particular family member, God. Imagine each of these persons in the dance with you. Then write about them in the light of these questions:*

1. Is your "touch" light? In which relationships do you cling?

2. How can you change the heavy-handed touch?

3. How are you nourished by the pattern of the rhythm of each relationship?

4. How do you set one another free for "the wingèd life"?

*Review each relationship in this light, especially your relationship to God.*

 *Saints for the Season*

JANUARY 28: SAINT THOMAS AQUINAS (ca. 1225–1274) is most famous for his great theological work, the *Summa Theologiae,* and his Scripture commentaries. Thomas has left the Church the legacy of vast writings, which have greatly influenced her teachings. Late in his life he had a mystical experience which so moved him that he was no longer able to write. He died on his way to the Second Church Council at Lyons. To celebrate the contribution of Saint Thomas, reflect today upon the presence of God, which pervades all of life.

# A World of Infinite Depth
### *Douglas Burton-Christie*

The desert elders had consciously looked to reduce the scope of their world, to sweep away all that was unnecessary and seek God in purity of heart. They retreated into the solitude and silence of the desert. They ruminated (literally chewed upon) the words of Scripture, steadily, faithfully, with great intensity, so that they might gradually be made over in their image. It was not necessary to multiply words. True, there are stories relating prodigious feats of memorization by certain elders. But more often, their attention was focused on a small group of psalms, or even a single word or phrase from Scripture. Retreat and rumination: These are words for the discipline and abandon that characterized the monks' radically simple approach to prayer. . . .

The desert elders were aware that to ruminate on a text in this way was to enter into a lifelong process of self-discovery. "There are times," Abba Isaac says, "when a [person] understands God's Scriptures with the clarity with which a surgeon understands the body when he opens up the marrow and veins. There are the times when our experience seems to show us the meaning by practical proof before we understand it intellectually." At such moments, we come to see the texts "reflected in the clear glass of our own moral experience." Eventually, a person's deep appropriation of Scripture becomes an "interior possession." Abba Nestoros describes it this way:

> If these things [from Scripture] have been carefully taken in and stored
> up in the recesses of the soul and stamped with the seal of silence, after-
> wards they will be brought forth from the jar of your heart with great
> fragrance; like some perennial fountain [they] will flow abundantly from
> the veins of experience and irrigating channels of virtue and will pour
> forth copious streams as if from some deep well in your heart.

This is experiential knowledge, the kind that comes only from long struggle and intense focus.

*JANUARY 31: SAINT JOHN BOSCO* (1815–1888) founded the religious order known today as the Salesians. This Italian Saint is noted for his work with homeless boys, for catechizing young people, and for his deep spirituality. To celebrate this feast you may wish to pray for young boys who are homeless or abused and to study some portions of the *Catechism of the Catholic Church.*

# *K*OINONIA: SOMETHING SHARED

### *Paul Lynd Escamilla*

The original Christian community was formed within the matrix of shared life— both in its persecution, mission, worship, and fellowship. One New Testament term for this "sharing" is *koinonia,* a rich word suggesting many meanings—partnership, community, participation, communion. Literally it means "sharing with someone in something," and it is used to refer to sharing with God and in Christ, as well as with others.

Beyond this specific New Testament word, we need not look far to discover the *koinonia* dimension of the entire biblical narrative. In the Gospels alone we see the washing of feet, the sharing of bread, the shedding of tears; we see a stranger befriended, a son reconciled to a father, a mother pleading on behalf of her sick daughter; we see Jesus touching blind eyes and withered limbs, enfolding children in his arms, looking a stranger in the eye and asking for water, charging his closest friend with denial, sweating blood in prayer, caring for his mother from the Cross.

It's no wonder, then, that when the church gathers to rejoin the biblical story in worship, the reality of *koinonia* comes to such palpable expression. We know such closeness to God and those around us when we harmonize a hymn, share the bread and cup, take each other's hand in passing the peace or saying hello, wink at a child peering over the next pew, speak our prayers of confession, wait together in silence, come to the altar rail for prayer or healing, receive a word of blessing. As we share with others in the worship of God, we become intimately bound up with God and one another in more ways than we know. . . .

To worship together is to participate in the intimacy of such a *koinonia,* with Christ as well as one another. We take part in the whispering, in the sharing of the word through song and verse and bread and silence, through tears and laughter, confession and delight—all as the means by which together we come to meet and know God.

The Bantus of South Africa have a saying that illumines the meaning of koinonia in worship: *umuntu, ngamuntu, ngabantu* ("a person is a person because of other persons"). Such a truth regarding identity and society applies naturally to worship as well: A worshiper is a worshiper because of other worshipers, and because of the stirring presence of God in that worship. The first fruit of our worship, then, is the intimate sharing with God and others in the very doing of worship, whether it be a hymn that we share, a cup, a prayer, or a whisper.

*Saints for the Season*

*FEBRUARY 1: SAINT BRIDGET* (ca. 450–525), patron of Ireland, is said to have been baptized by Saint Patrick in Kildare, where she established a monastery. This later became a double monastery of women and men. Think about all the contributions the Irish have made to Catholicism and honor Saint Bridget by baking some Irish soda bread today.

# CATHERINE OF SIENA
*Wendy M. Wright*

Catherine di Giacomo di Benincasa was the talk of her fourteenth-century Italian hometown. Twenty-fourth child of a well-to-do wool dyer and his wife, Catherine was notable in her youth for her intelligence and stubborn independence, traits that also characterized her later life. Refusing marriage in adolescence, she embarked on a regime of intense solitary prayer. In time she became attached to a group of pious women, the Mantellate, who were affiliated with the Dominicans but lived in their own homes. In her solitude, which was marked by extremes of asceticism and ecstatic experience, the young Catherine underwent what she termed a "mystical espousal" to Christ, from which issued a mandate to give herself in service to the poor and sick. Attracting groups of followers by the evident holiness of her life, Catherine became noted as a spiritual advisor. She also was an avid learner and imbibed much from the learned Dominicans with whom she was in contact. Another later striking experience, her "mystical death," signaled the beginning of new apostolic ventures. Drawn into the sociopolitical conflicts of the Italian city-states and the institutional chaos of that century's papacy, Catherine began to be a counselor and peacemaker. Sometimes successful in her efforts, sometimes betrayed by her unscrupulous allies, she continued to work vigilantly to reform what she considered to be the great scandals of Christendom: the decadence of the clergy and the flight of the papacy from Rome. The most lasting testimony of this woman's short but feverishly committed life (she died in 1380 at the age of thirty-three) is her Dialogue, a lengthy recording of her ecstatic five-day dialogue between "the soul who asks God four questions and the Lord Himself who replies to the soul, enlightening her with many useful truths."

. . . The intimate and reciprocal life of the mystical body Catherine depicted in the *Dialogue* in a passage where God is revealed as the eternal gardener.

Do you know what course I follow, once my servants have completely given themselves to the teaching of the gentle loving Word? I prune them, so that they will bear much fruit—cultivated fruit, not wild. . . .

These are the true workers. They till their souls well, uprooting every selfish love, cultivating the soil of their love in me. They feed and tend the growth of the seed of grace that they received in holy baptism. And as they till their own vineyards, so they till their neighbors' as well, for they cannot do the one without the other. . . .

You, then, are my workers. You have come from me, the supreme eternal gardener, and I have engrafted you onto the vine by making myself one with you.

Keep in mind that each of you has your own vineyard. But every one is joined to your neighbor's vineyards without any dividing lines. They are so joined together, in fact, that you cannot do good or evil for yourself without doing the same for your neighbors.

All of you together make up one common vineyard, the whole Christian assembly, and you are all united in the vineyard of the mystic body of holy Church from which you draw your life. In this vineyard is planted the vine, which is my only-begotten Son, into whom you must be engrafted.

---

*Reflect upon the life of Catherine and this passage from her* Dialogue *in a prayerful, centered way. You may choose to record the words of God to Catherine and listen to them as a centering meditation. God speaks these words to you!*

*In your journal write down the truths this reflection reveals to you. These questions may guide your reflection:*

1. How has God pruned you?

2. What action of tilling and cultivating will you take on?

3. How can you till the vineyard of your neighbor?

4. What does the image of a common vineyard evoke in you?

*Allow God's Spirit to inspire you as you write.*

*Saints for the Season*

FEBRUARY 3: *SAINT BLAISE* (d. ca. 316), who was martyred, was thought to have come from Armenia. Most of what we know of Blaise are legends, particularly regarding his helping to save a boy who was choking on a fish bone. Thus, Blaise is known for helping people with throat ailments. The blessing of throats on the Feast of Saint Blaise is a tradition that remains in most churches today. Today try to attend a local parish and have your throat blessed and pray for those with throat cancer, those who are unable to speak, and for any persons who are suffering with a throat problem.

# *I* NEED TO BREATHE DEEPLY

*Ted Loder*

Eternal Friend,
grant me an ease
to breathe deeply of this moment,
    this light,
        this miracle of now.
Beneath the din and fury
    of great movements
        and harsh news
            and urgent crises,
make me attentive still
    to good news,
        to small occasions,
            and the grace of what is possible
                for me to be,
                    to do,
                        to give,
                            to receive,
that I may miss neither my neighbor's gift
    nor my enemy's need.

Precious Lord,
grant me
    a sense of humor
        that adds perspective to compassion,
    gratitude
        that adds persistence to courage,
    quietness of spirit
        that adds irrepressibility to hope,
    openness of mind
        that adds surprise to joy;
that with gladness of heart
I may link arm and arm
with the One who saw signs of your kingdom
    in salt and yeast,
        pearls and seeds,
            travelers and tax collectors,
                sowers and harlots,
                    foreigners and fishermen,
and who opens my eyes with these signs
    and my ears with the summons
        to follow to something more
            of justice and joy.

 *Saints for the Season*

FEBRUARY 7: SAINT THOMAS MORE (1478–1535) was Chancellor of England during the turbulence of Henry VIII's reign. During his career, Thomas More was a humanist who struggled for social reform through the educational process. His works include *Utopia,* a social satire, and many letters, written during his imprisonment. Take time to look at the unjust social structures that exist in your community. Determine an action that you can undertake to make even a small change—boycotting, letter writing, contacting a senator.

# An Exercise in Loving

*Carol A. Gura*

Find a quiet time in your busy days to deal with the heart of Jesus' command to love, even your enemy. Sit in silence for a short time, ridding your mind of all distractions. Aware of your breathing and heartbeat, enter the deepest recesses of your being to encounter the living God. When you have arrived at that place, ask the Holy Spirit to guide you as you meditate.

As you breathe in the life of the Spirit, begin to repeat over and over again, "Love your enemies; do good to those who hurt you." As you exhale, breathe out all the pain and unforgiveness that has accumulated in your heart to be released. Continue this breathing and the words for as long as you need.

Allow the memory of a hurtful situation to arise in your subconscious. Imagine yourself in that situation, recalling the person who hurt you, your feelings, and the circumstances. Reimagine the situation again; this time, Jesus is with you, embracing you in your hurt—understanding your pain completely. As you feel the presence and embrace of the Lord, repeat, once again, the words "Love your enemies; do good to those who hurt you."

If you are able, recall the circumstances of your hurt one more time. This time look at the person who hurt you with the eyes of Jesus. Ask the Spirit to help you envision the pain, the anger, and the issues which caused this person to treat you so unjustly. Look into his or her eyes. Allow the love of Jesus to flood your being. Continue looking at your enemy with the loving eyes of Jesus. Allow the Holy Spirit to transform your feelings from fear and anger to love and compassion. Speak to this person with the compassion of Jesus.

Linger in this place as long as you are able, allowing God's loving embrace to include you and your enemy.

When you are ready, return to the room where you are meditating.

Then take up your journal and write about your experience. You may need to repeat this exercise of healing several times to allow the transforming grace of love and compassion to sink deeply into your heart. Don't rush your feelings; just allow God to work in you. It will also help to pray for your enemy each day.

 *Saints for the Season*

*FEBRUARY 11: OUR LADY OF LOURDES* is the feast celebrated to honor Mary's apparition to Bernadette at Lourdes, France. The miraculous spring, which came forth from the cave of Our Lady's apparition, continues today to be a source of healing for pilgrims who visit this site. Pray for all the sick today and allow this prayer to lead you to take action by visiting a sick relative, friend, or neighbor.

# BRIEFLY IT ENTERS, AND BRIEFLY SPEAKS

*Jane Kenyon*

I am the blossom pressed in a book
and found again after 200 years . . .

I am the maker, the lover, and the keeper . . .

When the young girl who starves
sits down to a table
she will sit beside me . . .

I am food on the prisoner's plate . . .

I am water rushing to the wellhead,
filling the pitcher until it spills . . .

I am the patient gardener
of the dry and weedy garden . . .

I am the stone step,
the latch, and the working hinge . . .

I am the heart contracted by joy . . .
the longest hair, white
before the rest . . .

I am the basket of fruit
presented to the widow . . .

I am the musk rose opening
unattended, the fern on the boggy summit . . .

I am the one whose love
overcomes you, already with you
when you think to call my name. . . .

As you meditate upon this poem this week, underline or highlight some of the images of God that speak to your life.

Take one of these images of God and use it as you pray. Journal your feelings as you pray in this manner.

When you have some time, take the poem, line by line, and write your response to that image of God, through the lens of one who is a follower—a disciple. In other words, what does this image of God evoke in you as a follower, one who is trying to imitate this vast mystery we call "God"?

## Saints for the Season

*JUNE 24: THE BIRTH OF JOHN THE BAPTIST,* the cousin of Jesus who prepared the way for the Messiah by his preaching a baptism of repentance, is written of in all the Gospels. Today read about John from any of the Gospel accounts and spend some time reflecting upon his life and mission.

# THE ANOINTING

*Carol A. Gura*

Knowingly or not, she prepared him for burial,
    that Mary-woman.
Timidly she approached him, tentative at first,
    not wanting to breach the customs of her day,
    not wanting to intrude—to violate his privacy.
But, compelled by love,
    love caught in the gaze,
    in the brush of his passing;
Love born out of a knowing look
    penetrated her soul
    and her body reacted—
Washing, anointing,
    readying Jesus for death.

Ann, like Mary, was timid and unsure.
But, her desire to express her love
    won out.
Love grown of long years of sharing:
    smiles, words, beds, meals.
Love sharing heavy burdens:
    pain, doubt, fear, betrayal,
but love nonetheless—
    love all the more took over
        that Saturday morning.

She moved slowly, hesitating, at first,
     covering his naked skeleton with
          the dignity of the dying,
     helping his frail frame into
          the baptismal waters of death-to-life.
Her eyes averted the cancer pallor of
     flesh hanging on the bones of the dying.
"Thin," she thought, "too thin,"
     wondering when
          death would make its claim.

Tenderly she washed,
     gently she spoke,
          carefully she prepared him.
When she finished the water ritual,
     he summoned up his last
          bit of strength to declare fiercely,

    "I'll shave myself!"
As she watched she knew she had to keep
     sacred the dignity of his dying,

to let go of her need to help;
     let go, let go of him,
        let go soon.

In the twilight of that eve of Sabbath,
     washed clean, shaven and clothed,
     he waited for her
        for death.
Alone and waiting,
     knowing or not, but waiting
        he sat.
Endless it must have been
     because the call was strong.
"What took her so long?"
     The final letting go was here.

She brought in the steamy soup.
Relieved, she had come at last.
They were waiting with him:
     twins, parents, friends all beckoned.

And, he heaved a sigh of relief,
     the waiting is over.
Washed clean, anointed in love
     he was ready to go home.

---

*As you reflect upon* The Anointing, *recall any experience you might have had with a sick or dying person. Describe this experience in the space provided. Try to imagine yourself in the situation of dying. These questions may guide your reflection:*

1. What would you be thinking and doing?

2. How would you want to prepare for your last day on earth?

3. What does your experience of death teach you about Baptism? About the resurrection of the body at the end of time?

*Saints for the Season*

*JUNE 29: SAINTS PETER AND PAUL, APOSTLES,* the two great leaders of the early Christian community, were both martyred for their faith, but not before establishing the foundations of Christianity in both the Jewish and the Gentile worlds. Today read sections of the Acts of the Apostles to follow their travels as they preached the Good News and established communities centered in the "breaking of the bread."

# *M*INDING THE CALL
### *Elaine M. Prevallet*

*T*here is no "typical" call. Other persons, no doubt more open-minded and willing than I, seem to experience their call in a gentler process, involving a gradual clarifying. Others make step-by-step choices, learning from their experience, heeding the counsel of mentors and friends, sorting and discerning. Commitment then becomes a kind of distilling process guided over a period of time by the Holy Spirit. The focus, too, of the call can differ. I name "the desire for God" as the grounding of my own call; others might name their calls in terms of a life of service, community, or the poor. A call might be such that it requires all one's life energies and a life commitment, or it might be, at a different level, a temporary call to service in a particular situation that lies as a burden on one's heart. Its temporary quality does not make it any less a call. For most, the call has a particular container—a marriage, a church community, a mission site. At the deepest level, the call *frees* us. It enables us to see what really matters, to focus our love, to dedicate ourselves to something/Someone larger than ourselves, and so to enter consciously into that continual stream of losing and finding ourselves that is the mystery of life. God uses a variety of ways to get through to us, tailoring the call to the condition of the recipient. No matter how the call comes, whether explosively or gently, the response has to be worked out in daily fidelity, in ordinary life. Keeping the focus in the midst of the seductive values of the culture becomes our life task. . . .

God only calls us to be who we are. By God's gift, our deepest identity is not really to *be* or to *do* anything but love. We are, each of us, the uniquely individual container of God's love in whatever particular context we life. We live to serve that love, to give it expression. The call to love is the same for everyone, unique for everyone. Our role is to help each other become free enough to entrust ourselves to the One who calls us.

In the end, we have no assurance, ever, that we have done it "right"; no assurance, that is, except the peace that comes when our lives have integrity, and the love that seems to open out once the obstacles are cleared. Even these are only hints and guesses. There will always be, deep within every human, the quiet pull of God's transcending "more" tugging at our hearts. The drawing of that love and the voice of that calling will stay steady.

 *Saints for the Season*

JULY 4: *SAINT ELIZABETH OF PORTUGAL* (1271–1336) is noted for her works of charity and peacemaking efforts as the queen of Portugal. Upon the death of her husband, she retired to live with the Poor Clares as a secular Franciscan until her death. Allow the spiritual model of this married leader of a country to be an inspiration to your own life in the Lord.

# *WALKING WITH JESUS*
### *Dolores R. Leckey*

My morning rituals have become as important to me as breathing. Coffee, the spectacle of sunrise (ever ancient ever new, I silently chant), *Washington Post* headlines, intercessory prayer, and a walking meditation. Lately I head into my urban neighborhood imagining I am in Galilee, part of a walking group that is accompanying Jesus. He's taking us through fields of poppies, saying, "Look at the flowers. Look at them. Don't pass them by." I check the traffic lights, cross some streets, turn a few corners, and then I hear Jesus singing:

*The Road goes ever on and on*
*Down from the door where it began.*
*Now far ahead the Road has gone,*
*And I must follow, if I can,*
*Pursuing it with weary feet,*
*Until it joins some larger way,*
*Where many paths and errands meet.*
*And whither then? I cannot say.*

We, the imagined walkers, all join in the song. The historical Jesus would not have known Tolkien's work, of course, but in the world of imagination all things are possible, and we can walk and sing with Jesus, listening for his directions, pursuing the mystery of the road.

---

*One morning this week take this walk with Jesus and see the world through his eyes. Journal what you see. Reflect upon the poem from J.R.R. Tolkien's* The Fellowship of the Ring *and allow it to speak to your experience of following Jesus. Write some of the parallels between your life and the poem in your personal journal.*

 *Saints for the Season*

JULY 14: SAINT KATERI TEKAKWITHA (1656–1680), also known as "Lily of the Mohawks," survived the smallpox epidemic that took the lives of her parents and was eventually baptized into the Catholic faith. When she refused to marry, she had to flee her people. She lived a life of charity and holiness at the Mission of Saint Francis Xavier near Montreal, Canada. Learn more about the Native Peoples and their contributions to Christianity and our more ecological worldview today.

# THE ROOTS OF INTERPERSONAL AND SOCIAL CONFLICT

*Thomas E. Clarke*

Whence this strange mixture of wound and blessing, blessing and wound, in the relationship of individual and community? I suggest that it is rooted in what traditionally has been called original sin, what today some describe as "the sin of the world." It is a fungus growth, a parasite clinging to the created image of God in each of us, guaranteeing that faithfulness to God on the part of both individual and community will lead to situations of impasse and conflict. Still more will unfaithfulness on the part of one or both partners result in conflict. By the same token I would say that the wise and courageous facing up to such conflict is integral to our experience of the paschal mystery. When both individual members and the community are willing to die to preconceived false images of what the relationship is meant to be, the darkness can be transformed. Poor Lazarus emerges from the tomb and is unbound.

For all of his deficiencies, personal and ideological, the great Augustine profoundly grasped how deeply human beings are wounded in their entry into the world. He saw that humanity is wounded at its heart, namely that rich and complex drama in which a man and a woman come together and together become with God cocreators of the human future. The dualistic flaws of his philosophy and the intrusion of his personal anxieties into his vision of sin and grace have preoccupied commentators, at times blinding them to what is brilliant and enduring in his account of the human condition.

Modern psychology, I believe, has in effect put plausible flesh on Augustine's abstract portrayal. Beneath the classic nature-nurture quarrel, it has reached a broad consensus regarding the roots of interpersonal and social conflict. A man and a woman, each bringing from the family of origin a heritage of blessings and wounds, join their energies in the procreative and nurturing process that we call family. Inevitably, in diverse forms and varying degrees, there is generated in their offspring the whole panoply of pressures, constraints, and enabling opportunities that are grist for the mill of the self-making process. And just as inevitably there emerges the contest happily described by both psychologists and spiritual writers as the struggle between the false self and the true self.

Often the contest is described in such a way that community and society emerge as "the bad guy," threatening the innocent individual, whose sole strategy must consist in resisting the threat from without. Such a scenario, I believe, oversimplifies the contest, and hinders the victory of the true self. It misses the melancholy truth that early on we all become complicit with our own betrayal. It also neglects what is grace and blessing in the energies exercised by communities toward their members. The source of our wounds remains the source of our blessings. If "family is forever," as a therapist friend frequently reminds me, its potential is for weal as well as for woe. Where sin abounds, grace abounds yet more.

*Saints for the Season*

*JULY 22: SAINT MARY MAGDALENE,* follower of Jesus, is probably the Mary, healed of demons (Luke 8:2), to whom the Risen Jesus appeared on Easter morning. As such she was the first disciple commissioned to "tell" the Good News of Jesus' Resurrection from death. Many scholars believe that Mary Magdalene was the leader of an early Christian community. Read about Mary's conversion and her presence at the Cross and Resurrection scenes in the Gospels. Determine how you can take the Good News to others as she did, even in the face of disbelief.

# THE MIRACLE
*Boris Pasternak*

He was walking from Bethany to Jerusalem,
Brooding over sad premonitions.

The sun scorched the slope's prickly shrubs,
No smoke was rising over a nearby hut,
The air was hot and the reeds motionless,
And the calm of the Dead Sea lay still.

And with a bitterness rivalling the sea's,
He walked with a small throng of clouds
Along a dusty road, to somebody's backyard,
On His way to a gathering of disciples.

And so immersed was He in His thoughts,
That the field, dejected, sent off a wormwood smell.
All was still. He stood alone in the midst of it,
While the land lay prostrate in swoon.
All became muddled; the heat, the desert,
The lizards, the springs, the streams.

A fig tree rose not too far off,
Fruitless, nothing but branches and leaves.
And He said to it: "Of what use are you?
What joy does your stupor bring me?

"I thirst and hunger, yet you stand barren,
My meeting you is joyless as granite.
O, how offensive and ungifted you are!
Remain as you are, then, till the end of time."

A tremor of condemnation ran through the tree,
Like a spark of lightning down a rod.
The fig tree was reduced to ashes.

If only a moment of freedom had been given
To the leaves, the branches, roots, trunk,
The laws of nature could have intervened.
But a miracle is a miracle, and a miracle is God.
When we're in confusion, in the midst of disorder,
It overtakes us instantly, by surprise.

## Saints for the Season

_JULY 31: SAINT IGNATIUS OF LOYOLA_ (1491–1556), a layman and soldier, underwent a radical religious conversion while recovering from wounds sustained in the defense of Pamplona. Following that transformation he spent a year as a beggar and wrote _The Book of Spiritual Exercises,_ a work explaining how to meditate on Scriptures, grow in faith, and discern God's will. Read more about the life of Ignatius to celebrate his feast today.

# FORGIVING AND EXCUSING

### C. S. Lewis

Forgiving does not mean excusing. Many people seem to think it does. They think that if you ask them to forgive someone who has cheated or bullied them you are trying to make out that there was really no cheating or no bullying. But if that were so, there would be nothing to forgive. They keep on replying, "But I tell you the man broke a most solemn promise." Exactly: that is precisely what you have to forgive. (This doesn't mean you must necessarily believe his next promise. It does mean that you must make every effort to kill every trace of resentment in your own heart—every wish to humiliate or hurt him or to pay him out.) The difference between this situation and the one in which you are asking God's forgiveness is this: In our own case we accept excuses too easily, in other people's we do not accept them easily enough. As regards my own sins it is a safe bet (though not a certainty) that the excuses are not really so good as I think: as regards other men's sins against me it is a safe bet (though not a certainty) that the excuses are better than I think. One must therefore begin by attending carefully to everything which may show that the other man was not so much to blame as we thought. But even if he is absolutely fully to blame we still have to forgive him; and even if 99 percent of his apparent guilt can be explained away by really good excuses, the problem of forgiveness begins with the 1 percent of guilt which is left over. To excuse what can really produce good excuses is not Christian charity; it is only fairness. To be a Christian means to forgive the inexcusable, because God has forgiven the inexcusable in you.

This is hard. It is perhaps not so hard to forgive a single great injury. But to forgive the incessant provocations of daily life—to keep on forgiving the bossy mother-in-law, the bullying husband, the nagging wife, the selfish daughter, the deceitful son—how can we do it? Only, I think, by remembering where we stand, by meaning our words when we say in our prayers each night "Forgive our trespasses as we forgive those that trespass against us." We are offered forgiveness on no other terms. To refuse it is to refuse God's mercy for ourselves. There is no hint of exceptions and God means what He says.

 *Saints for the Season*

*AUGUST 8: SAINT DOMINIC* (1170–1221) founded the Order of Preachers, the Dominicans, during the course of his efforts in fighting the heresy of Albigensianism in southern France. This band of preachers, priests, and nuns traveled on foot to take the Word of God to the people of France and northern Italy. Reflect upon the role of good preaching in your own spiritual growth. Pray for those called to the ministry of preaching in your local Church, that the light of truth might guide them.

# FIRE ON THE EARTH
### *Macrina Wiederkehr*

I have come to light a fire
on the earth
Oh how I wish
the flames
were already leaping.

Yes, there is a Baptism
awaiting me
How distressed I feel
until it is accomplished.

After a statement like that
from a Person like that
I still allow the fire of my life
to be a simple glimmer
instead of a flame.

That Baptism he struggled with . . .
I, too, walk around it
instead of *into it*
into the flame
where death
waits for me,
only, to show me
the face of life.

Jesus wrestled with the fire
but he didn't walk around the flames
He plunged into the fire
    into the flames
    into the death
When he came out
it was Resurrection
and his anguish turned to joy.

I am called to the same vocation
the same bath of fire waits for me,
the same God calls out to me:
    I placed you here
    to light a fire on the earth
    Oh how I wish the flames
    were already leaping
    But you have a baptism
    to receive
    and like me
    you'll be restless
    until it's over.

*Reflect this week upon the fire that Jesus has placed within you. Describe the ways you have experienced the leaping flames of this fire. You may choose to brainstorm some ways you can light this fire on the Earth as did Jesus. Look over your ideas and choose one way you can change from a "simple glimmer" to a person "on fire" for Jesus.*

 *Saints for the Season*

*AUGUST 11: SAINT CLARE* (1193–1253), companion of Saint Francis, committed her life to following the Gospel and living the rigorous poverty of Francis. She is said to have sealed her commitment with the cutting of her long, beautiful hair, her most prized possession. She served as superior of her companions (including her mother and two sisters), who became known as the Poor Clares. Continue to reflect upon simplifying your life by taking action to give one of your treasured possessions to another.

# GESTALT AT SIXTY

*May Sarton*

How rich and long the hours become,
How brief the years,
In this house of gathering,
This life about to enter its seventh decade.

I live like a baby
Who bursts into laughter
At a sunbeam on the wall,
Or like a very old woman
Entranced by the prick of stars
Through the leaves.

And now, as the fruit gathers
All the riches of summer
Into its compact world,
I feel richer than ever before,
And breathe a larger air.

I am not ready to die,
But I am learning to trust death
As I have trusted life.
I am moving
Toward a new freedom
Born of detachment,
And a sweeter grace—
Learning to let go.

I am not ready to die,
But as I approach sixty
I turn my face toward the sea.
I shall go where tides replace time,
Where my world will open to a far horizon.

Over the floating, never-still flux and change.
I shall go with the changes,
I shall look far out over golden grasses
And blue waters. . . .

There are no farewells.

Praise God for His mercies,
For His austere demands,
For His light
And for His darkness.

———————————————

*As you read and think about this poem, recall the riches of your own life. Name these blessings aloud as you sit and meditate.*

*Close your eyes and imagine your own death. What new freedom does this letting go bring to you? Then write of this experience of looking death in the eyes and the feelings you encountered in this meditation.*

*Reflect upon the changes you are facing and about the far horizon that awaits you. What action seems to be required of you at this time? Write your ideas in your journal.*

 *Saints for the Season*
———————————

*AUGUST 14: SAINT MAXIMILIAN KOLBE* (1894–1941) was a Polish Franciscan who volunteered to be executed in place of a young father while imprisoned in a Nazi concentration camp. Celebrate the feast of this contemporary Saint by examining the violence in your own life. Resolve to take on more nonviolent ways of dealing with others.

# At Last, Her Laundry's Done

*Kathleen Norris*

Laundry seems to have an almost religious importance for many women. We groan about the drudgery but seldom talk about the secret pleasure we feel at being able to make dirty things clean, especially the clothes of our loved ones, which possess an intimacy all their own. Laundry is one of the very few tasks in life that offers instant results, and this is nothing to sneer at. It's also democratic; everyone has to do it, or figure out a way to get it done. . . .

Of course an attachment to laundry can be pathetic, even pathological, in a woman who feels that it's one of the few areas in her life over which she has control. More often, though, it's an affectionate throwback to the world of our mothers and grandmothers. We may be businesswomen or professors, but it's hard to shake that urge to do laundry "the right way," just like mama did. The sense that "laundry must not be done casually," as an arts administrator once told me, is something that seems lost on most men. . . .

Living in the house where she [my mother] grew up, I've become pleasantly haunted by laundry. I'm grateful that I no longer have to pull clothes through a wringer, as my grandmother did for years. Her bottles of blueing gather dust in the basement; I haven't used them, but can't throw them out. But, like her, I wouldn't dream of using the electric dryer unless I have to. In March or April I begin to long for the day when I can hang clothes on the line again. Our winters are so long and severe in western South Dakota that we bank on the slightest summer joys; the scent of clothes dried out of doors, the sweet smell of sun on them.

---

*As you read this passage, allow your memory to wander back in time to your mother, grandmother, and other women of your family and the routines they developed for taking care of the ordinary tasks around the house, like the laundry. Journal some of these memories.*

*Continue your reflection by responding to these questions:*

1. What does the action of washing dirty clothes clean again symbolize for you?

2. How can doing the laundry become a time of prayer?

3. What do this passage and your memories reveal about your spiritual journey?

*Saints for the Season*

*AUGUST 15: THE ASSUMPTION OF THE BLESSED VIRGIN MARY* into Heaven is today's feast, a holy day that honors the beauty of Mary's life and her death, whereupon she was taken up into Heaven, body and soul. This doctrine of the Church offers us assurance in the grace of God, which overcomes all evil and death itself. Celebrate the harvest of Mary's life by serving a meal of freshly harvested foods to friends and family.

# THE FOUNTAIN

*Denise Levertov*

Don't say, don't say there is no water
to solace the dryness at our hearts.
I have seen

the fountain springing out of the rock wall
and you drinking there. And I too
before your eyes

found footholds and climbed
to drink the cool water.

The woman of that place, shading her eyes,
frowned as she watched—but not because
she grudged the water,

only because she was waiting
to see we drank our fill and were
refreshed.

Don't say, don't say there is no water.
That fountain is there among its scalloped
green and gray stones,

it is still there and always there
with its quiet song and strange power
to spring in us,
up and out through the rock.

_Read_ The Fountain _several times; then close your eyes and place yourself inside the poem. Imagine this fountain, springing out of the rock wall. Imagine yourself climbing up to get at the refreshing water. Think about the dryness in your life, the need for refreshment. Who is the woman who makes sure you are filled and renewed? Now imagine this fountain within yourself, always present, always refreshing. What is the rock that needs to break open for it to spring up in you? In writing of your experience of the fountain, name some of the people who wish to come to drink at the fountain of your life. How can you, like the woman in the poem, make sure all are filled and refreshed?_

_When you have finished your meditation, write about your feelings and insights in your personal journal._

*Saints for the Season*

*AUGUST 21: SAINT PIUS X* (1835–1914), a contemporary Pope, is noted for his lowering the age of First Holy Communion to the age of discretion, about age seven. His Eucharistic reforms and personal sanctity are cause for us to celebrate the gift of presence the Catholic Church has in the modern world today.

# THE SONS OF MARTHA
### *Rudyard Kipling*

The Sons of Mary seldom bother, for they have inherited that good part;
But the Sons of Martha favour their Mother of the careful soul and the troubled heart.
And because she lost her temper once, and because she was rude to the Lord her Guest,
Her Sons must wait upon Mary's Sons, world without end, reprieve, or rest.

It is their care in all the ages to take the buffet and cushion the shock.
It is their care that the gear engages; it is their care that the switches lock.
It is their care that the wheels run truly; it is their care to embark and entrain,
Tally, transport, and deliver duly the Sons of Mary by land and main.

They say to mountains, "Be ye removed." They say to the lesser floods, "Be dry."
Under their rods are the rocks reproved—they are not afraid of that which is high.
Then do the hill-tops shake to the summit—then is the bed of the deep laid bare.
That the Sons of Mary may overcome it, pleasantly sleeping and unaware.

They finger death at their gloves' end where they piece and repiece the living wires.
He rears against the gates they tend: they feed him hungry behind their fires.
Early at dawn, ere men see clear, they stumble into his terrible stall,
And hale him forth like a haltered steer, and goad and turn him till evenfall.

To those from birth is Belief forbidden; from these till death is Relief afar.
They are concerned with matters hidden—under the earth-line their altars are—
The secret fountains to follow up, waters withdrawn to restore to the mouth,
And gather the floods as in a cup, and pour them again at a city's drouth

They do not preach that their God will rouse them a little before the nuts work loose.
They do not teach that His Pity allows them to drop their job when they dam'-well choose.
As in the thronged and the lighted ways, so in the dark and the desert they stand.
Wary and watchful all their days that their brethren's days may be long in the land.

Raise ye the stone or cleave the wood to make a path more fair or flat—
Lo, it is black already with blood some Son of Martha spilled for that!
Not as a ladder from earth to Heaven, not as a witness to any creed,
But simple service simply given to his own kind in their common need.

And the Sons of Mary smile and are blessed—they know the Angels are on their side.
They know in them is the Grace confessed, and for them are the Mercies multiplied.
They sit at the Feet—they hear the Word—they see how truly the Promise runs.
They have cast the burden upon the Lord, and—the Lord He lays it on Martha's Sons!

 *Saints for the Season*

*AUGUST 23: SAINT ROSE OF LIMA* (1586–1617) was the first canonized Saint of the Americas and is the patron of South America and the Philippines. Rose is noted for modeling her life on Saint Catherine of Siena and is said to have had extraordinary mystical gifts. To honor Saint Rose, take time today to pray in a silent, contemplative style. This style of prayer clears the mind and heart to complete silence, making room for God to change and speak to our hearts.

# THE SEEKER

*Mary Lou Sleevi*

Around the house
there is always This Broom
in a room.
Usually women push it . . .
diligently.

This Woman puts fine focus
on a spot on the floor . . .
directing lamplight,
enlarging its sphere.
She is credited with an Eye for Detail.

Women identify the worker
in particularly personal terms,
"She's like a sister to me."
And oh, those miscellanies
—like little plastic pieces—
under The Broom!

In a world that's a zone of disordered time,
a litany of "Just a Minute!"
sets the standard for a day.

So much that is longed for
can't be reached in
just a minute.

The undervalued Coin she seeks
may be to her
a pearl of great price.

She can name it
by herself.
She may name it
herself.

With eyes trained on the job,
her Broom stalks the floor
she walks every day.

In a corner, so to speak,
between the memorable and memorized
parables of Jesus
about a lost sheep and a prodigal son,
is a Metaphor for God
less impressed on Mother Church.

> "'What woman,
> if she has ten silver pieces
> and loses one,
> does not light a lamp
> and sweep the house
> in a diligent search
> until she has retrieved what she lost?

> "'And when she finds it,
> she calls in her friends and neighbors
> to say,
> 'Rejoice with me!
> I have found the silver piece
> I lost!'

> "'I tell you,
> there will be the same kind of joy
> before the angels of God
> over one repentant sinner.'"

The scriptural Image reflects on
a common ground of Experience.
"What woman does not . . ." do these things?
asks the opening verse. . . .

Women's search for identity
closely relates to Hunger for God.
She struggles
to be a real person in her world.
She has to be.

Beyond the miscellanies
(under a broom that is sometimes plastic)
what's real about me, God?
What's real about you?

That's the Risk of the Broom
and the Fear of the Dark.

God does not light the wick;
I do.
Good God, why *me?*

Because you will do these things,
speaks from the heart.

You reach for the stars
with your eyes on Good Earth.

---

*As you reflect upon this poem ask yourself: What is "The Broom"? The "undervalued coin"? How do these symbols reflect your "Hunger for God"? Your own "search for identity"? Read the poem several times and write your own reflection in the space provided. Think about women who have no coins or identity, women who are alienated from the Church because of their lifestyle or culture. What can you do to reach out to reconcile these women? Write down your ideas for taking action, and when you do act, note your experience of outreach.*

 *Saints for the Season*

*AUGUST 27: SAINT MONICA* (331–387) was a North African woman who worked with the poor while raising her family. She is noted for her patient prayers for her son, Augustine, whose dissolute lifestyle was a constant disappointment. Before her death she witnessed his conversion through the witness of Ambrose, the bishop of Milan. Pray today for those family members who are caught in the lure of the culture and have forgotten their spiritual growth.

# Our Daily Bread

*Cèsar Vallejo*

Breakfast is drunk down . . . Damp earth
of the cemetery gives off the fragrance of the precious blood.
City of winter . . . the mordant crusade
of a cart that seems to pull behind it
an emotion of fasting that cannot get free!

I wish I could beat on all the doors,
and ask for somebody; and then
look at the poor, and, while they wept softly,
give bits of fresh bread to them.
And plunder the rich of their vineyards
with those two blessed hands
which blasted the nails with one blow of light,
and flew away from the Cross!

Eyelash of morning, you cannot lift yourselves!
Give us our daily bread,
Lord . . . !

Every bone in me belongs to others;
and maybe I robbed them.
I came to take something for myself that maybe
was meant for some other man;
and I start thinking that, if I had not been born,
another poor man could have drunk this coffee.
I feel like a dirty thief . . . Where will I end?

And in this frigid hour, when the earth
has the odor of human dust and is so sad,
I wish I could beat on all the doors
and beg pardon from someone,
and make bits of fresh bread for him
here, in the oven of my heart . . . !

*AUGUST 28: SAINT AUGUSTINE* (354–430), son of Monica, had the greatest influence on Western Christianity after his conversion. His many writings include the famous *Confessions,* an autobiographical account of the soul's search for God. Read a portion of the *Confessions* to celebrate the legacy of Saint Augustine.

# SAINT AUGUSTINE'S CONFESSIONS
### Wendy M. Wright

Written in mid-life, the *Confessions* chronicles the North African saint's journey from childhood through his conversion to Christianity in his thirty-second year. Along the way the reader is compelled by the story of his youthful education in the classical tradition, his intense yet complex relationship with his devout mother, his early peer-driven "crimes," his ambivalent attachment to women, including the lower-class mistress who bore his son, his zealous pursuit of life's meaning through his affiliation with the religious sect of the Manichees, his scrutiny of Neo-Platonic philosophy and finally, his exploration of and conversion to Christianity.

Always the probing, restless thinker, Augustine sifts through the artifacts of his personal history to find there the insistent action of God, drawing him closer through events that, in the happening, seemed to have little to do with divine presence. For the North African, the art of remembering is not photographic recall; it is a creative, instructive, and formative undertaking. He comes to know and love God through the evidence of God-with-him in the concrete particularities of his personal history.

On another level, the *Confessions* is also a remembering of a vaster kind. As Augustine crafts the narrative of his life from hindsight, he creates an almost archetypal Christian portrait of the human person's movement into God. The inner dynamic of the story shows the young Augustine acting first out of an attitude of "superbia" (pride or self-centeredness) and gradually coming to embrace a posture of "humilitas" (humility or God-centeredness). The boy Augustine is motivated by a grasping ambition to possess wealth, status, love, even spiritual wisdom. His gradual conversion involves learning to let go, to become a recipient, to cease using "the beautiful things of this world" for his own narrow purposes. He redirects desire to the source of beauty, God. Augustine, in so remembering his story, remembers as well the overarching story of Christianity in which the central archetypal figure, Jesus, is one who gains his true life by losing it, who empties himself to become the one who embodies the God-centered life for all humankind. So the *Confessions* weaves together the great and little stories of Christ and the saint with the threads of personal and communal memory.

 *Saints for the Season*

SEPTEMBER 8: THE NATIVITY OF THE BLESSED VIRGIN MARY is celebrated today. Her parents, Anne and Joachim, long childless, were overjoyed at the birth of their only child, a daughter. Today remember those who are struggling to conceive a child. Offer encouragement and prayer to those childless couples you might know.

# FEAR AND ANGER REDEEMED
### *Thomas E. Clarke*

Imagine some interpersonal conflict in which, knowingly or not, someone puts you down. At the first stage your fear is great and controlling, and your anger has not been unleashed so that you might deal with the assault on your dignity. Your posture is one of *submissiveness*. You acquiesce. You conform. In effect, you put yourself down. You accept victimhood. To an unknowing spectator you might give the impression of a virtuous humility. In fact you are participating in the denial of your human dignity.

But now suppose that, by God's grace and your own incipient courage, you reduce the controlling influence of your fear. Your adrenaline begins to flow more freely as the sturdier of the twins begins to play a role, however awkwardly and immaturely. You are led to retaliate in a sneaky way. Against the effort of another to put you down you are prompted to try to put them down. Let us call this posture hostility. You will feel badly about it, but perhaps not as badly as you felt about your previous submissiveness. Believe it or not, you are making progress in or towards virtuous action. You don't need to become perfect all at once.

At the third stage, aggressiveness, your anger finally comes out of the closet, reducing still more the domination of your fear. You lash out, perhaps, repelling the assault on your dignity, but not yet with full maturity, so that you attack openly the dignity of your assailant. You do unto another as that other has done unto you. Now both your adversary and any onlookers become uncomfortable, fearing real violence. You, however, experience a new satisfaction because your behavior matches your inner feelings. Once again, it is important not to retreat from this less-than-perfect posture. You are no longer dominated by fear, and your anger is out in the open where you can deal with it. You are on the right path.

The fourth and final stage, assertiveness, represents the fullness of the process of growth. Fear and anger, those precious psychospiritual energies, are still operative but have gradually become integrated and brought within the free commitment of your faith, hope, and love. They have not so much been overcome as redeemed and transformed into patience, courage, and hope. Patience and courage are themselves twin virtues, one more receptive, one more active in dealing with evil. Patience sticks it out, bears the yoke, endures, without either rebelling or collapsing. Courage carries the assault against the foe, braves danger and wounding in active pursuit of what is right and good.

Hidden within the virtues of patience and courage are the ugly ducklings, playing their humble but indispensable roles. Without fear, courage and patience lose their meaning. We are courageous only in the face of that which makes us afraid. And anger provides courage and patience with a certain toughness and sturdiness. We shall not be moved. We shall overcome. Who shall separate us from the love of Christ?

One thing that attracts me to this model of growth in virtue is the way it corresponds to the philosophy and discipline of nonviolent resistance to evil. Gandhi and many other exemplars of patience and courage in the face of injustice have made major contributions to spirituality in our day. I remember seeing a video some years ago that told the story of the four U.S. women who had been brutally murdered by the military in El Salvador. The final scene depicted a missioning ceremony at Maryknoll, New York, motherhouse of the missionary community founded by Mollie Rogers and James Walsh in the early twentieth century. Two Maryknoll sisters, Ita Ford and Maura Clarke, had been among the four victims. As the ritual reached its peak, lay missionaries came forward to receive the cross of mission. Among them was a married couple, with child in arms. The music was "Be Not Afraid," a song of the St. Louis Jesuits. The poignancy of that scene still lives in my memory. More eloquently than any words, it speaks the message of the Gospel that our fears and our angers need not be wasted on trivia or passively repressed. When we find ourselves paralyzed by one or rendered powerless by the other, we need to remember that these ugly ducklings are gifts, bestowed by a loving God who invites us always to patience, courage, and hope.

*Saints for the Season*

*SEPTEMBER 30: SAINT JEROME* (ca. 340–420), following a dream, devoted himself to a life of asceticism and biblical study. He established a monastery at Bethlehem and with the support of Paula, a wealthy disciple, he translated the Old Testament from the Hebrew into Latin. Honor this Doctor of the Church today by reading and reflecting on one of the Old Testament books.

## WELCOME MORNING

*Anne Sexton*

There is joy
in all:
in the hair I brush each morning,
in the Cannon towel, newly washed,
that I rub my body with each morning,

in the chapel of eggs I cook
each morning,
in the outcry from the kettle
that heats my coffee
each morning,
in the spoon and the chair
that cry "hello there, Anne"
in the godhead of the table
that I set my silver, plate, cup upon
each morning.

All this is God,
right here in my pea-green house
each morning
and I mean,
though often forget,
to give thanks,
to faint down by the kitchen table
in a prayer of rejoicing
as the holy birds at the kitchen window
peck into their marriage of seeds.

So while I think of it,
let me paint a thank-you on my palm
for this God, this laughter of the morning,
lest it go unspoken.

The Joy that isn't shared, I've heard,
dies young.

---

*As you read* Welcome Morning, *underline or highlight those images that speak to your heart. Make a list in your journal of those simple pleasures that bring you joy in the ordinary routines of your day.*

*In prayer ask yourself: For what do I wish to give thanks? Write your own poem of thanks for the simple things we all take for granted, lest it go unspoken, lest the "Joy . . . dies young."*

## Saints for the Season

OCTOBER 1: SAINT THÉRÈSE OF THE CHILD JESUS (1873–1897), also known as the Little Flower, entered the Carmelite monastery of Lisieux at the age of fifteen. There she suffered from tuberculosis and became a mystic. Her concept of the "little way" invites all to place unlimited hope on God's merciful love. Read some of Thérèse's works and reflect upon how grace—God's limitless love—has changed your life into something extraordinary.

# THE ESCAPE FROM COURAGE
### W. Paul Jones

Most theologians agree that the "feel" of existence is anxiety. Acknowledged or not, to be finite is in each moment to dangle over the abyss of nothingness as a "primitive terror." Such diagnoses as cancer, AIDS, or even the skip of a heartbeat, evoke a painful intimacy with our fragility. This is frightening, and "human kind cannot bear very much reality." We try to escape, on the one hand, by projecting our anxiety onto persons or groups we can then subjugate or destroy. Ethnics, gays, and women are favorite scapegoats. Even though the human mind is a permanent factory of idols (Calvin), escape is never permanent. There is always some other nation, corporation, party, group, or referee to trigger our primal insecurity. When paranoia regarding others is unsuccessful, our blame is projected inward into neurosis as an aversion to one's self. On and on goes the vicious circle.

This is why courage, the only adequate resolution of our primal predicament, is the road less taken. Courage requires a steadfast, honest gaze at the human condition, but we are paralyzed by the thought of doing it *alone*. Isolated we come into the world, and isolated we will leave, no matter how many persons are present. We experience this specter of primal loneliness either as the fear of rejection (the isolation of not belonging) or as the fear of ridicule (the isolation of not measuring up). Either way, this forces us to try to impress or please others. As we have seen, this road most traveled leads inevitably to domestication and submissiveness—the opposite of courage.

Courage can be awakened only when we experience our dilemma as rooted neither in others nor ourselves, but in the fabric of existence itself. This is why faith is the only adequate courage—it enables us to resist self-deception and live in the full face of life as tragic. Christian courage is the treasure always contained in earthen vessels: "We are afflicted in every way, but not crushed; perplexed, but not driven to despair; persecuted, but not forsaken; struck down, but not destroyed; always carrying in the body the death of Jesus" (2 Cor. 4:8–10).

But how does Christian courage function if it does not explain away suffering or settle for compensatory rewards? *Faith is the courage to act as if we were not cosmically alone.* But such courage is not of our own making, not some grim, lip-biting obstinacy. Rather, it is rooted in a trusting heart, a heart confidant that in Christ, God so enters the struggle of life with death that the ongoing Divine/human crucifixion can be lived under the hope of resurrection. Christian courage is the heart of faith experienced as trust. *Courage* and *encourage* are related words, a fact revealed when my daughter, frightened to take her first dive, called out, "Courage me, Daddy." I made the only response she needed: "It's okay, I'm here with you." So Paul characterizes faith as courage: "Who shall separate us from the love of Christ? Shall tribulation, or distress, or persecution, or famine, or nakedness, or peril, or sword?" (Rom. 8:35). . . . This is the faith that bequeaths a courage that can face all things. God and all of us are in it together.

 *Saints for the Season*

OCTOBER 4: *SAINT FRANCIS OF ASSISI* (1181–1226) is the founder of the Franciscans and patron of animals. Many stories and legends abound about Francis's experiences and miracles, but the primary focus of his life was his dedication to "Lady Poverty." Read something about Saint Francis today and examine your life with a view toward simplifying it by letting go of material possessions.

# EAGLE POEM
### Joy Harjo

To pray you open your whole self
To sky, to earth, to sun, to moon
To one whole voice that is you.
And know there is more
That you can't see, can't hear
Can't know except in moments
Steadily growing, and in languages
That aren't always sound but other
Circles of motion.
Like eagle that Sunday morning
Over Salt River. Circled in blue sky
In wind, swept our hearts clean
With sacred wings.
We see you, see ourselves and know
That we must take the utmost care
And kindness in all things.
Breathe in, knowing we are made of
All this, and breathe, knowing
We are truly blessed because we
Were born, and die soon, within a
True circle of motion,
Like eagle rounding out the morning
Inside us.
We pray that it will be done
In beauty.
In beauty.

*Highlight or underline the phrases and images in this poem that touch on your experience of prayer.*

*Read the poem again, imagining the swooping, circling motion of the eagle, and breathe in the images of the poem. As you bring a petition to God in prayer, open yourself to discover what this request requires of you. Allow God to change you.*

*Now write about this experience, describing the circle of your life as it is revealed in your prayer of intercession.*

 *Saints for the Season*

OCTOBER 15: SAINT TERESA OF JESUS (Teresa of Ávila, 1515–1582), the first woman Doctor of the Church, founded the Discalced Carmelites (a reform convent of Carmelites) and was a great mystic. Among her works are *The Interior Castle, The Way of Perfection,* and *Meditations on the Song of Songs.* This Spanish mystic was adviser to many and friend of Saint John of the Cross. Read one of Teresa's works to honor her today.

# MOON SHELL

*Anne Morrow Lindbergh*

Moon shell, who named you? Some intuitive woman I like to think. I shall give you another name—Island shell. I cannot live forever on my island. But I can take you back to my desk in Connecticut. You will sit there and fasten your single eye upon me. You will make me think, with your smooth circles winding inward to the tiny core, of the island I lived on for a few weeks. You will say to me "solitude." You will remind me that I must try to be alone for part of each year, even a week or a few days; and for part of each day, even for an hour or a few minutes in order to keep my core, my center, my island-quality. You will remind me that unless I keep the island-quality intact somewhere within me, I will have little to give my husband, my children, my friends or the world at large. You will remind me that woman must be still as the axis of a wheel in the midst of her activities; that she must be the pioneer in achieving this stillness, not only for her own salvation, but for the salvation of family life, of society, perhaps even of our civilization.

---

*After reading this passage from* Gift from the Sea, *close your eyes and imagine yourself on the beach or any favorite place that has been a place of centering for you. Allow yourself to drink in the sights, sounds, and smells of that place. Allow God to come to you in that place.*

*When you have finished, write your experience of centering and imagining in the space provided. Take time to relax and imagine yourself in this place of healing and comfort several times over the next week and month.*

 *Saints for the Season*

OCTOBER 18: SAINT LUKE, author of one of the Gospels and the Acts of the Apostles, was a Syrian physician and companion of Saint Paul. It is believed that Luke wrote and died in Greece. He is patron of doctors, butchers, and artists. Celebrate this Evangelist's feast by reading the Gospel of Luke and continue by reading the Book of Acts.

# CONTEMPLATION AND COMMUNION

*Elizabeth A. Johnson*

Contemplation is a way of seeing that leads to communion. The fact that the world is simply there, in splendor and fragility, gives rise to wonder, leading to a religious sense of the loving power that quickens it. "The world is charged with the glory of God," exclaims poet Gerard Manley Hopkins, echoing the ancient psalmist's praise that "The heavens are telling the glory of God" (Ps 19:1). In contemplation the human spirit learns to see the presence of the divine in nature, and so recognizes that the earth is a sacred place. For such a spirit the biblical bush still burns, and we take off our shoes.

Through contemplation the religious spirit grows in the realization of how deeply humanity is embedded in the earth. We begin to know this experientially, to feel in the depths of our being that we are part of the living cosmos. Consequently, we recover a capacity for subjective communion with the earth. We develop what Barbara McClintock, the Nobel prize-winning biologist, calls "a deep feeling for the organism," which is a result of recognizing that we are all kin, related through ontological participation in the community of creation. Consequently, reciprocity rather than rape marks our approach. We reach out toward the earth not just with utilitarian intent, although that is appropriate within limits, but with non-violent appreciation for its own inherent value. The naturalist Louis Agassiz epitomizes this stance with his remark, "I spent the summer traveling. I got halfway across my backyard."

To the contemplative spirit, the vivifying power of God flashes out from the simplest natural phenomenon, the smallest seed. "Speak to the earth and it will teach you," Job urges his ignorant but well-meaning friends (Job 12:7). "Look at the birds of the air" and "consider the lilies of the field," Jesus teaches his disciples, knowing that they will find their testimony to God's care (Mt. 6:25–33). Earth, in a word, is a sacrament. Pervaded and encircled by the Creator Spirit it effects by signifying the subtly active presence of the holy giver of life. Without the knowledge of contemplation, which is akin to prayer, prophetic action on behalf of the earth will in the long run fall short of the wisdom needed for its long-term cherishing.

---

*Be sure to get out and experience nature this week. When you do, read this passage slowly and prayerfully. Jot down all the ways you feel connected to the natural world, to God, and to others. Think about changes that you might make in your lifestyle in order to live in deeper communion with God's gift of the created world.*

*Write your ideas in your personal journal. Check each day to evaluate your progress in developing a deeper kinship with the earth.*

 *Saints for the Season*

OCTOBER 19: SAINTS ISAAC JOGUES AND JOHN DE BREBEUF (1607–1646 and 1593–1649) were both French Jesuit missionaries and are patron Saints of Canada. Isaac Jogues brought the Gospel to the Hurons along Lake Superior and later traveled to the Mohawks, where a hatchet blow from an Iroquois warrior who thought he was a sorcerer killed him. Brebeuf, who lived among the Huron tribe for fifteen years, was captured and tortured to death when the Iroquois attacked the tribe. Read and reflect more about the Christianization of Native Peoples in North America. Offer some act of repentance or atonement for the errors held by the missionaries whose good intentions destroyed their culture.

# AN INTERRUPTED LIFE
*Etty Hillesum*

SUNDAY MORNING PRAYER. "Dear God, these are anxious times. Tonight for the first time I lay in the dark with burning eyes as scene after scene of human suffering passed before me. I shall promise You one thing, God, just one very small thing: I shall never burden my today with cares about my tomorrow, although that takes some practice. Each day is sufficient unto itself. I shall try to help You, God, to stop my strength ebbing away, though I cannot vouch for it in advance. But one thing is becoming increasingly clear to me: that You cannot help us, that we must help You to help our-selves. And that is all we can manage these days and also all that really matters: that we safeguard that little piece of You, God, in ourselves. And perhaps in others as well. Alas, there doesn't seem to be much You Yourself can do about our circumstances, about our lives. Neither do I hold You responsible. You cannot help us but we must help You and defend Your dwelling place inside us to the last. There are, it is true, some who, even at this late stage, are putting their vacuum cleaners and silver forks and spoons in safe keeping instead of guarding You, dear God. And there are those who want to put their bodies in safe keeping but who are nothing more now than a shelter for a thousand fears and bitter feelings. And they say, 'I shan't let them get me into their clutches.' But they forget that no one is in their clutches who is in Your arms. I am beginning to feel a little more peaceful, God, thanks to this conversation with You. I shall have many more conversations with You. You are sure to go through lean times with me now and then, when my faith weakens a little, but believe me, I shall always labour for You and remain faithful to You and I shall never drive You from my presence."

---

*An Interrupted Life is a passage taken from the diary of Etty Hillesum, a young Dutch Jewish woman, who recorded her spiritual awakening through the horrible days of the Nazi terror. Eventually she was taken to a concentration camp and died in Auschwitz on November 30, 1943. She gave her diaries to friends for safekeeping and eventually they were presented to the public in 1981. This remarkable faith journey offers us a life worthy of our reflection, especially today.*

 *Saints for the Season*

*NOVEMBER 1: THE SOLEMNITY OF ALL SAINTS* points to our desire to join with the Saints who have already died and are with God. Today we celebrate with the Church the joy and communion that exist between all those Saints and holy people who have already died and all people still living in the world. Choose a Saint whose life you can relate to and learn more about this holy one as you try to imitate his or her example of sanctity.

# $\mathcal{S}$EEDS OF CONTEMPLATION

*Thomas Merton*

$\mathcal{E}$very moment and every event of every man's life on earth plants something in his soul. For just as the wind carries thousands of winged seeds, so each moment brings with it germs of spiritual vitality that come to rest imperceptibly in the minds and wills of men. Most of these unnumbered seeds perish and are lost, because men are not prepared to receive them: for such seeds as these cannot spring up anywhere except in the good soil of freedom, spontaneity, and love.

This is no new idea. Christ in the parable of the sower long ago told us that "The seed is the word of God." We often think this applies only to the word of the Gospel as formally preached in churches on Sundays (if indeed it is preached in churches any more!). But every expression of the will of God is in some sense a "word" of God and therefore a "seed" of new life. The ever-changing reality in the midst of which we live should awaken us to the possibility of an uninterrupted dialogue with God. By this I do not mean continuous "talk," or a frivolously conversational form of affective prayer which is sometimes cultivated in convents, but a dialogue of love and of choice. A dialogue of deep wills.

In all the situations of life the "will of God" comes to us not merely as an external dictate of impersonal law but above all as an interior invitation of personal love. Too often the conventional conception of "God's will" as a sphinx-like and arbitrary force bearing down upon us with implacable hostility, leads men to lose faith in a God they cannot find it possible to love. Such a view of the divine will drives human weakness to despair and one wonders if it is not, itself, often the expression of a despair too intolerable to be admitted to conscious consideration. These arbitrary "dictates" of a domineering and insensible Father are more often seeds of hatred than of love. If that is our concept of the will of God, we cannot possibly see the obscure and intimate mystery of the encounter that takes place in contemplation. We will desire only to fly as far as possible from Him and hide from His Face forever. So much depends on our idea of God! Yet no idea of Him, however pure and perfect, is adequate to express Him as He really is. Our idea of God tells us more about ourselves than about Him.

We must learn to realize that the love of God seeks us in every situation, and seeks our good. His inscrutable love seeks our awakening. True, since this awakening implies a kind of death to our exterior self, we will dread His coming in proportion as we are identified with this exterior self and attached to it. But when we understand the dialectic of life and death we will learn to take the risks implied by faith, to make the choices that deliver us from our routine self and open to us the door of a new being, a new reality.

The mind that is the prisoner of conventional ideas, and the will that is the captive of its own desire cannot accept the seeds of an unfamiliar truth and a supernatural desire. For how can I receive the seeds of freedom if I am in love with slavery and how can I cherish the desire of God if I am filled with another and an opposite desire? God cannot plant His liberty in me because I am a prisoner and I do not even desire to be free. I love my captivity and I imprison myself in the desire for the things that I hate, and I have hardened my heart against true love. I must learn therefore to let go of the familiar and the usual and consent to what is new and unknown to me. I must learn to "leave myself" in order to find myself by yielding to the love of God. If I were looking for God, every event and every moment would sow, in my will, grains of His life that would spring up one day in a tremendous harvest.

*Saints for the Season*

*NOVEMBER 2: ALL SOULS* commemorates those who have died with Christ as their hope for new and eternal life in God. The belief that there is a time of purification after death, that our good works and prayers help the dead, and that there is an intermediary place between Heaven and hell, are all the focus of today's feast. Today remember in a prayerful way those loved ones who have died.

# NOW AND AGAIN

*Lawrence Recla*

There is a grey time of day,
   now,
      when the fog is in
         and the tide is out,
            when even the surf
               is more feeble.

When blue is a real
   state of mind
      and a hoped for
         state of sky.

When color is
   but in small flowers.
When lilies but bud
   floating on a small pond
      by steep stairs
         to the sea.

When reality is dull
   and there is more pulsing
      amid the kelp beds
         than through my veins.

When bees are about their blooms
　　with more dedication
　　　　than I muster for any joy.
When my prayer
　　is but this pause.
When my praying
　　is only my ears and eyes
　　　　for my mouth is mute.

I await
　　thy pleasure,
　　　　Oh my God.
Banish the bluntness of my hopes.
Quicken me to bliss
　　that I may better weather
　　　　days like these
　　　　again.

 *Saints for the Season*

NOVEMBER 3: SAINT MARTIN DE PORRES (1579–1639) was a Dominican lay brother who cared for the sick and for slaves in Lima, Peru. He is the patron of interracial justice. Honor Martin today by reflecting upon your own racial prejudices. Resolve to take action to change your inner attitudes.

# Our Faith Is a Light

*Julian of Norwich*

Our faith is a light, coming in nature from our endless day, which is our Father, God; in which light our Mother, Christ, and our good Lord the Holy Spirit lead us in this passing life. This light is measured with discretion, and it is present to us in our need in the night. The light is the cause of our life, the night is the cause of our pain and all our woe, in which woe we deserve endless reward and thanks from God; for we by his mercy and grace willingly know and believe our light, walking therein wisely and mightily. And at the end of woe, suddenly our eyes will be opened, and in the clearness of our sight our light will be full, which light is God, our Creator, Father, and the Holy Spirit, in Christ Jesus our saviour.

So I saw and understood that our faith is our light in our night, which light is God, our endless day.

---

*One evening this week sit alone in a dark room and recall those dark times in your life. Then light a candle and watch the ways the flickering light illuminates the room. Think about those times that you have experienced the light of faith.*

*Spend as much time as you need, reflecting in silence. When you have finished, write about the light of faith in your experience.*

*Think about those who need the light of faith, those who are experiencing dark times. Resolve to bring your light into their darkness in a nonintrusive and gentle way.*

*Saints for the Season*

*NOVEMBER 11: SAINT MARTIN OF TOURS* (ca. 316–397), born to pagan parents, became a catechumen at the age of twelve, took a military oath at age fifteen, and was baptized when he was eighteen. In Gaul, Martin became a monastic and established a community there for which he is heralded as the founder of Western monasticism. Many miracles and legends are attributed to Saint Martin. Learn more about the monastic movement, which has had a profound influence on the Church.

# *T*HE BUTTERFLY EFFECT
## *Madeleine L'Engle*

*B*ut everything we are learning about the nature of Being is making it apparent that "us" versus "them" is a violation of Creation. Tribalism must be transformed into community. We are learning from astrophysics and particle physics and cellular biology that all of Creation exists only in interdependence and unity.

In a recent article on astrophysics I came across the beautiful and imaginative concept known as "the butterfly effect." If a butterfly winging over the fields around Crosswicks should be hurt, the effect would be felt in galaxies thousands of light years away. The interrelationship of all of Creation is sensitive in a way we are just beginning to understand. If a butterfly is hurt, we are hurt. If the bell tolls, it tolls for us. We can no longer even think of saying, "In the Name of the Lord will I destroy them." No wonder Jesus could say that not one sparrow could fall to the ground without the Father's knowledge.

Dr. Paul Brand points out that every cell in the body has its own specific job, in interdependence with every other cell. The only cells which insist on being independent and autonomous are cancer cells.

Surely that should be a lesson to us in the churches. Separation from each other and from the rest of the world is not only disaster for us, but for everybody from whom we separate ourselves. We must be very careful lest in insisting on our independence we become malignant.

If we take the whole sweep of the story, rather than isolating passages out of context, this is the message of Scripture. So now, as we take the next steps into the wilderness into

which God is sending us; now, as the human creature has moved from being the primitive hunter to the land-worker to the city-dweller to the traveller in the skies, we must move on to a way of life where we are so much God's own people that warfare is no longer even a possibility. It is that, or disaster, and we must not let Satan, the great separator, win.

The phrase, "the butterfly effect," comes from the language of physics. It is equally the language of poetry, and of theology. For the Christian, the butterfly has long been a symbol of resurrection.

The butterfly emerges from the cocoon, its wings, wet with rebirth, slowly opening, and then this creature of fragile loveliness flies across the blue vault of sky.

Butterflies and angels, seraphim and cherubim, call us earth-bound creatures to lift up our mortal dust and sing with them, to God's delight.

Holy. Holy. Holy!

*As you reflect on* The Butterfly Effect, *recall some of the beautiful butterflies you have seen. Imagine their movements and think about their connection to your life and the life of the planet. Journal your thoughts about the beautiful symbol of the butterfly.*

*Think about a time when you felt the connection that Madeleine describes and that astrophysics affirms. Write about that time in the space provided. How will you act more responsibly, knowing that all that you do affects the entire universe? Note your resolution and track your efforts to change.*

 *Saints for the Season*

*NOVEMBER 13: SAINT FRANCES XAVIER CABRINI* (1850–1917), the first U.S. citizen canonized a Saint, was born in Lombardy, Italy. There she established a religious congregation and was invited by the archbishop of New York to work in the United States. There Frances and her five companions established hospitals, orphanages, schools, and convents. Celebrate the work of Mother Cabrini by volunteering to visit the sick in your parish.

# *T*HE DIVORCE OF HEAVEN AND HELL
## C. S. Lewis

*B*lake wrote the *Marriage of Heaven and Hell.* . . . In some sense or other the attempt to make that marriage is perennial. The attempt is based on the belief that reality never presents us with an absolutely unavoidable "either-or"; that, granted skill and patience and (above all) time enough, some way of embracing both alternatives can always be found; that mere development or adjustment or refinement will somehow turn evil into good without our being called on for a final and total rejection of anything we should like to retain.

This belief I take to be a disastrous error. You cannot take all luggage with you on all journeys; on one journey even your right hand and your right eye may be among the things you have to leave behind. We are not living in a world where all roads are radii of a circle and where all, if followed long enough, will therefore draw gradually nearer and finally meet at the center: rather in a world where every road, after a few miles forks into two, and each of those into two again, and at each fork you must make a decision. Even on the biological level life is not like a pool but like a tree. It does not move towards unity but away from it, and the creatures grow further apart as they increase in perfection. Good, as it ripens, becomes continually more different not only from evil but from other good.

I do not think that all who choose wrong roads perish; but their rescue consists in being put back on the right road. A wrong sum can be put right: but only by going back till you find the error and working it afresh from that point, never by simply going on. Evil can be undone, but it cannot "develop" into good. Time does not heal it. The spell must be unwound, bit by bit, "with backward mutters of dissevering power"—or else not. It is still "either-or." If we insist on keeping Hell (or even earth) we shall not see Heaven: if we accept Heaven we shall not be able to retain even the smallest and most intimate souvenirs of Hell.

I believe, to be sure, that any man who reaches Heaven will find that what he abandoned (even in plucking out his right eye) was precisely nothing: that the kernel of what he was really seeking even in his most depraved wishes will be there, beyond expectation, waiting for him in "the High Countries." In that sense it will be true for those who have completed the journey (and for no others) to say that good is everything and Heaven everywhere. But we, at this end of the road, must not try to anticipate that retrospective vision. If we do, we are likely to embrace the false and disastrous converse and fancy that everything is good and everywhere is Heaven.

But what, you ask, of earth? Earth, I think, will not be found by anyone to be in the end a very distinct place. I think earth, if chosen instead of Heaven, will turn out to have been, all along, only a region in Hell: and earth, if put second to Heaven, to have been from the beginning a part of Heaven itself.

*Saints for the Season*

*NOVEMBER 18: SAINT ROSE PHILIPPINE DUCHESNE* (1769–1852), French missionary and educator, established a convent of the Religious of the Sacred Heart in Saint Charles, Missouri. The Potawatomi tribe, among whom she worked, called her the "Woman Who Prays Always." Take time during the course of each day to "pray always."

# HELP ME TO BELIEVE IN BEGINNINGS

*Ted Loder*

God of history and of my heart,
so much has happened to me during these whirlwind days:
    I've known death and birth;
    I've been brave and scared;
    I've hurt, I've helped;
    I've been honest, I've lied;
    I've destroyed, I've created;
    I've been with people, I've been lonely;
    I've been loyal, I've betrayed;
    I've decided, I've waffled;
    I've laughed and I've cried.
You know my frail heart and my frayed history—
and now another day begins.

O God, help me to believe in beginnings
and in my beginning again,
no matter how often I've failed before.

Help me to make beginnings:
    to begin going out of my weary mind
        into fresh dreams,
            daring to make my own bold tracks
                in the land of now;
    to begin forgiving
        that I may experience mercy;
    to begin questioning the unquestionable
        that I may know truth;
    to begin disciplining
        that I may create beauty;
    to begin sacrificing
        that I may accomplish justice;
    to begin risking
        that I may make peace;
    to begin loving
        that I may realize joy.

Help me to be a beginning for others,
　　　to be a singer to the songless,
　　　a storyteller to the aimless,
　　　a befriender of the friendless;
　to become a beginning of hope for the despairing,
　　　of assurance for the doubting,
　　　of reconciliation for the divided;
　to become a beginning of freedom for the oppressed,
　　　of comfort for the sorrowing,
　　　of friendship for the forgotten;
　to become a beginning of beauty for the forlorn,
　　　of sweetness for the soured,
　　　of gentleness for the angry,
　　　of wholeness for the broken,
　　　of peace for the frightened and violent of the earth.

Help me to believe in beginnings,
　　　to make a beginning,
　　　　to be a beginning,
　so that I may not just grow old,
　　　but grow new
　each day of this wild, amazing life
　　　you call me to live
　　　　with the passion of Jesus Christ.

 *Saints for the Season*

NOVEMBER 22: SAINT CECILIA dedicated her life to prayer, fasting, and virginity, even as a young child. Her arranged marriage to Valerian did not daunt her holy vows. Her father respected her chosen way and she remained a virgin, opening her home to those in need of prayer and spiritual direction. She was martyred and is honored as the patron of music because her heart was full of song for God. Listen to a lovely piece of music today in honor of Saint Cecilia.

# Steps on the Journey

# Steps on the Journey

As a people we hunger to
  mark our passage into new realms
  in ways
      that celebrate and reclaim our true identity.
The process of initiation,
  the journey of conversion,
  has its own markers and milestones—
      memory maps of the sacramental tradition found in
Catholicism.

Acceptance or welcome speaks
  loud and clear, "You are embraced in love!"

Election tells of our "chosen" place,
  "You are no longer strangers and aliens!"

Freedom from sin and darkness, open to the light of grace.
  The community prays, Scrutinies,
      for the elect, for itself.
  We are exorcised of all that keeps us apart
      from God, from one another.
Purified we are awakened from our sleep,
  our thirst, our blindness, our tombs
to be enlightened by the Light of Christ.

All these encounters with the Risen One;
  present in the Word, the people gathered,
in the prayers, in the laying on of hands.

Rituals celebrated in the midst of God's people
    connect us
        one to each other,
for in them we encounter the living Christ!

Milestones marking the journey toward fullness
    in the Body of Christ:
Baptized, plunged into the death waters,
    rising to new life;
Sealed and confirmed in the Spirit's
    empowering gifts,
        anointed for mission;
Ready to be Eucharist for the world,
    the Body of Christ
        broken and poured out for life itself.

Let us mark these Steps on the Journey
    with reverence,
    with eyes and ears open wide,
    with hearts that are eager and ready!

Carol A. Gura

# Preparing for the Rite of Acceptance

As you prepare for the Rite of Acceptance into the Order of Catechumens, or the Rite of Welcoming if you were baptized in another faith tradition, take the time to prepare. Set aside some quiet time this week to pray and reflect. This process will guide you as you prepare.

---

A. *Begin by reading this poem:*

## FINDING THE RIVER
### Carol Gura

Pilgrims and pioneers
    Searched the landscape
    To find their way
To where?
    The place of promise—
        The river of life.

Along the way;
    Great walls
        Needed scaling and tearing down;
Let go of the burdens that fill your
    Hands and hearts
Let go!

Along the way;
    The path curved and twisted
        Lost in death's grip
Let go of your false pride
    Your idols and ego,
Let go!

Along the way;
   Thorny, densely tangled mats
      Of confusion and doubt;
Let go of the voices of the past
   That block and bind,
Let go!

Along the way;
   Death lurks beneath
      Denied, delusions of mortality
Let go
   Round the corner
   For the river you seek
Lies at your feet.

---

B. *As you reflect upon this poem, think about your own pursuit, your own search for God—for a community of faith. These questions will guide your thoughts:*

1. What walls needed scaling or tearing down when you decided to begin this process?

2. What unexpected twists and turns brought you to this spiritual place?

3. Name some of the confusion and/or doubt that remain as you continue this journey.

4. What do you seek in this river of life?

---

C. *Take time to write your story of coming to inquire about the Catholic faith and what has happened since.*

D. *Read and ponder John 1:29–42, which shares with us the story of two disciples' response upon seeing Jesus:*

Jesus turned and saw them [the disciples] following him and said to them, "What are you looking for?" They said to him, "Rabbi" (which translated means Teacher), "where are you staying?" He said to them, "Come, and see."

*John 1:38–39a*

E. *Place yourself in the scene and reread the passage. Imagine that Jesus is asking you, "What are you looking for?"*

1. What feelings arise in you as you hear Jesus' invitation: "Come, and you will see"?

2. In what way is God inviting you to move deeper and deeper in your journey of faith?

# Reflecting on the Rite of Acceptance

A.  *Begin your time of quiet by finding a still space and an uninterrupted time of day. Light a candle and pray the prayer used in your Rite of Acceptance or Rite of Welcome:*

You have followed God's light and the way of the Gospel now lies open before you. Set your feet firmly on that path and acknowledge the living God, who truly speaks to everyone. Walk in the light of Christ and learn to trust in his wisdom. Commit your lives daily to his care, so that you may come to believe in him with all your heart.

*Rite of Acceptance, 52*

B.  *Close your eyes and recall your experience of the ritual. Some key moments of this rite are listed below. Recall, once again, these moments as you experienced them and the feelings they invoked in you. Now write in your journal about your reaction and your experience:*

Gathering with your sponsor

The community's welcome

Expressing what you desire from God and from the Catholic community

Accepting the Gospel as a way of life

Being signed with the cross

Listening to God's Word

Being presented with God's Word

Being prayed for by the community

Being sent forth from the community with the Word and a catechist

C. *Take time to allow this meditation to sink into your heart and soul:*

# $\mathcal{M}$EDITATIONS WITH HILDEGARD OF BINGEN
### *Hildegard of Bingen*

$\mathcal{T}$he soul is kissed by God
in its innermost regions.

With interior yearning,
grace and blessing
are bestowed.

It is a yearning to take on God's
gentle yoke,
it is a yearning to give one's self
to God's way.

D. *Write your response to these questions:*

1. How has this process been a blessing and a grace for you?

2. What has changed in your life?

3. What is God's "gentle yoke" you yearn to take on?

4. What will you do to give yourself to God?

E. *Write a prayer or a poem or just some thoughts that express your response to God's "kissing your soul."*

# Preparing for the Rite of Election _____

$\mathscr{A}$s you prepare for the important Rite of Election, take some time this week to ready your heart to take this next step on your journey toward full initiation.

_____

A. *Find a quiet place, and allow the Word of God in this passage to enter into the deepest part of your being:*

For once you were darkness, but now in the Lord you are light. Live as children of light—for the fruit of the light is found in all that is good and right and true. Try to find out what is pleasing to the Lord.

*Ephesians 5:8–10*

_____

B. *Recall the many months of preparation up to this point. During these months God's Word has been forming, molding, and challenging you. God's light has grown brighter in you. Your own faithfulness to God and to what pleases God has deepened in you. Write about your experience of God's light piercing the dark recesses of your soul.*

*C. Pray this poem:*

# THE PRAYER OF ONE READY FOR BIRTH
*Macrina Wiederkehr*

O God who creates something
    out of nothing
Compassionate shaper of clay
Tiller of the soil
Midwife God
I am ready to be born.

I'm giving up the darkness
    of the womb.
I'm waiting for the life
    that you alone can give.
A little light
    slipped through a crack
    last night
and covered up my fears.

A promise
    leaned against my heart
    last night
and told me it was mine.

And you were in that promise, Lord
And you were in the light.
It's enough to give me hope again.
I'm giving up the night.

D. *As you ready yourself to set your heart totally on Christ and fully desire to be initiated through the Sacraments of Baptism, Confirmation, and Eucharist, write your response to the following:*

1. The darkness I have let go of or turned away from is . . .

2. Signs of God's light and promise in me are . . .

3. I am ready to be born because . . .

4. I am giving up the night because . . .

# Reflecting on the Rite of Election

A. *Begin your time of quiet by finding a still space and an uninterrupted time of day. Light a candle and pray the prayer used in your Rite of Election.*

In God's name and on behalf of the Church the bishop states:

"I now declare you to be members of the elect,
  to be initiated into the sacred mysteries at the next Easter Vigil."

RCIA 133

---

B. *Close your eyes and recall your experience of the ritual. Some key moments of this rite are listed below. Recall, once again, these moments as you experienced them and the feelings they evoked in you. Now write about your reaction and your experience:*

Gathering with the assembly in the Church

Listening to God's Word

Hearing your sponsor speak on your behalf

Signing the book of the elect

Gathering with all the other catechumens and candidates of the diocese at the cathedral

Being presented to the bishop by name or through your parish's book of the elect

Hearing the bishop's declaration that you are elect, chosen by God

C. *Take time to allow this meditation to sink into your heart and soul:*

# THE PRAYER OF ONE BURSTING WITH LIFE

*Macrina Wiederkehr*

Jesus
Tree of Life
Your roots have found me
I am bursting with life
I feel like a brand new bud
singing gratefully to you
I will awaken the world
with the silent song of my being
My voice is not needed
I will preach
the gospel of silence
joyfully
as I burst forth
hopefully
into the sacred space
of this new day
knowing full well
this is only a pale glimmer
of the Life I am becoming
SO FULL OF LIFE AM I!

D. *Write your response to these questions:*

1. How has Jesus found you?

2. What metaphors or images describe your joy at this stage in the journey?

3. What is the new life that fills your being?

E. *Sit in prayer with these words for several minutes:*

[You are] God's chosen ones, holy and beloved.

*Colossians 3:12*

*Then say silently as you breathe in, "I am holy," and as you exhale, "chosen by God." Repeat this breathing prayer over and over again.*

F. *When you have finished, write a few words or phrases in your journal to describe how it feels to know that you are holy, beloved, and chosen by God.*

# Reflecting on the First Scrutiny

*T*HIRD SUNDAY OF LENT

---

A.  Take time this week to reflect on your experience of the
Scrutiny. Begin by finding a quiet place. Bring a clear pitcher
of water to help you focus during this time of prayer. Allow
the words of this poem to enter the depths of your heart:

## *B*REAKING
*Wendell Berry*

*D*id I believe I had a clear mind?
It was like the water of a river
flowing shallow over the ice. And now
that the rising water has broken
the ice, I see that what I thought
was the light is part of the dark.

---

B.  Ask yourself these questions and then write your response:

1.  What is the "rising water" in you that has broken the ice?

2.  How would you describe the darkness that has come to
light?

3.  How has your mind been cleared through this Scrutiny?

C.  *Read and ponder John 4:4–42. Place yourself into the scene at the well and listen as Jesus speaks these words to you:*

"Everyone who drinks of this water will be thirsty again, but those who drink of the water that I will give them will never be thirsty. The water that I will give will become in them a spring of water gushing up to eternal life." . . .

Then the woman left her water jar and . . . said to the people, "Come and see a man who told me everything I have done!" . . .

*John 4:13–14, 28–29*

D.  *Close your eyes and remember your experience of the Scrutiny. Write about that experience, including your feelings at various times during the ritual. Close by describing the way you experience Christ as "living water" for you.*

E.  *Now sit in prayer for five or ten minutes. Imagine a fountain of water, Christ, springing up within you, filling you, and flowing over you. Speak the prayer of your heart to Christ.*

# Reflecting on the Second Scrutiny

*F*OURTH SUNDAY OF LENT

---

A. *Take time this week to reflect on your experience of the Scrutiny. Begin by finding a quiet place. Light a candle as the focus of your meditation. Allow the words of this poem to enter the depths of your heart:*

## *T*O KNOW THE DARK
### *Wendell Berry*

*T*o go in the dark with a light is to know the light.
To know the dark, go dark, go without sight,
and find that the dark, too, blooms and sings.
And is traveled by dark feet and dark wings.

---

B. *Ask yourself these questions and then write your response:*

1. When have you gone "without sight"?

2. What dark feet and wings have been parts of your dark times?

3. How has the light of this Scrutiny opened your eyes to "know the light"?

C. *Read and ponder John 9:1–41. Place yourself into the story of the healing of the man blind from birth. Listen as Jesus speaks these words to you:*

"I am the light of the world." When he had said this, he spat on the ground and made clay with the saliva, and spread the clay on his eyes. . . . [The man] went and washed, and came back able to see. . . .

Jesus . . . said, "Do you believe in the Son of Man?" . . . He said, "I do believe, Lord." . . . Jesus said, "I came into this world for judgment, so that those who do not see might see, and those who do see might become blind."

*John 9:5–7, 35, 38, 39*

D. *Close your eyes and remember your experience of the Scrutiny. Write about that experience, including your feelings at various times during the ritual. Close by describing the spiritual blindness that you choose to turn over to the healing touch of Jesus.*

E. *Sit in silent prayer. Close your eyes and imagine the light of Christ filling your head, heart, and whole body. See this light expand and brighten in you. After a few moments, speak to Christ about the light and sight you desire.*

# Reflecting on the Third Scrutiny _____

FIFTH SUNDAY OF LENT

_____

A. Take time this week to reflect on your experience of the last
   Scrutiny. Begin by finding a quiet place. Bring a seed and a
   flower to help you focus your time of prayer. Allow the words
   of this poem to enter the depths of your heart:

## THE BROKEN GROUND
### Wendell Berry

The opening out and out,
body yielding body:
the breaking
through which the new
comes, perching
above its shadow
on the piling up
darkened broken old
husks of itself:
but opening to flower
opening to fruit opening
to the sweet marrow
of the seed—
   taken
from what was, from
what could have been.
What is left
is what is.

B. *Ask yourself these questions and then write your response:*

1. What has broken open in you as you prepare for full communion in the Catholic community?

2. What "husks" of your life have yielded to the flowering of your faith?

3. How does "What is left is what is" describe you?

C. *Read and ponder John 11:1–45. Place yourself in the crowd at the tomb of Lazarus. As Jesus speaks these words to Martha, you know he says them directly to you. As Jesus calls to Lazarus, he calls you:*

"I am the resurrection and the life. Those who believe in me, even even though they die, will live, and everyone who lives and believes in me will never die." . . . [Jesus] cried with a loud voice, "Lazarus, come out!" . . . Jesus said to them, "Unbind him, and let him go."

*John 11:25–26, 43, 44*

D. *Close your eyes and remember your experience of the Scrutiny. Write about that experience, including your feelings at various times during the ritual. Close by describing those parts of you that have kept you bound and how you can leave them behind in the tomb.*

E.   *Now sit in quiet prayer with Christ. Imagine Christ taking you by the hand and leading you freely away from any old hurts and patterns of life that entomb you. See Christ and others remove the cloths that have bound and burdened you. Imagine yourself emerging from the tomb with Christ in freedom and fullness of life. After a few moments, speak the prayer in your heart to Christ.*

# Preparing for
# Baptism, Confirmation, and Eucharist

## The Easter Vigil

Spend some time alone this week in a quiet place where you can take the time to prepare for full initiation into the Catholic community by receiving the Sacraments of Baptism (except those already baptized), Confirmation, and Eucharist.

---

A. *As you prepare to enter the baptismal waters, or to renew your Baptism, consider the following:*

The early Christians turned toward the west, the place of darkness, and stated that they detach themselves from sin and anything that holds them back from Christ.

*Write down those things from which you want to separate and leave behind in the baptismal waters. Then, like the early Christians, stand, face the west, and name these things aloud, saying: "I detach myself from. . . ."*

---

B. *Now think about this early Church practice:*

The early Christians then turned toward the east, the place of the rising sun, and stated that they attach themselves to Christ.

*Write down how you can abide in and attach yourself to Christ. Then, like the early Christians, stand, face the east, and state: "I attach myself to you, Christ, by. . . ."*

C. *Now sit and center your thoughts on the Sacrament of Confirmation with the help of this reflection:*

# Sealed in the Spirit

*Carol A. Gura*

You ready yourself
for sealing—baptismal seal—of Confirmation.
The Spirit—the *ruah*—
    the breath is stirring,
      God's breath
        blows where it will.
Don't you feel it,
    smell it in the air?
Born again of water and the Spirit,
    the Spirit that filled
      Jesus of Nazareth.
This same Spirit is ruffling at the corners of your soul.
Will you let the Spirit come?
It takes great courage and faith
    to breathe in the Holy Spirit.
Breathe in now and allow this wind of God to
    blow freely through your whole being.

D. *Sit quietly and breathe in the Spirit. As you breathe in, whisper, "Fill me" and as you breathe out, "O Spirit." After several minutes change the words as you breathe in to "Empower me," continuing with, "O Spirit," as you breathe out.*

E. *Consider this poem reflection as you anticipate the Sacrament of Eucharist:*

## BROKEN AND SHARED
*Carol A. Gura*

Blessed and broken,
    bread of threshed grains
Blessed and poured out,
    blood of crushed grapes.
You are willing to be
    broken, poured out, and shared.

I am willing to taste and see
    your goodness.
I am ready to be broken
    and poured out
      and shared.
For your nourishing Life will sustain me
    in the breaking,
      in the pouring out,
        in the sharing.
You lure me on,
"Taste and see the bread of life;
drink the blood by which you live in me."

F. *Allow these words to permeate your being. Close your eyes and reflect upon what it means to be broken, poured out, and shared. Think about how you will be Eucharist for the world. Then write about your thoughts, expressing your longing to be in communion with Christ and the Catholic community.*

# Reflecting on Initiation

## The Easter Vigil

After your full initiation into the Catholic faith community, take time to be alone and allow the full effect of this wondrous experience to transform your life.

---

A. *In a quiet place begin by prayerfully reflecting upon this prayer from the liturgy of the Easter Vigil:*

All-powerful God, Father of our Lord Jesus Christ,
by water and the Holy Spirit
you freed your sons and daughters from sin
and gave them new life.

Send your Holy Spirit upon them
to be their helper and guide.

Give them the spirit of wisdom and understanding,
the spirit of right judgment and courage,
the spirit of knowledge and reverence.
Fill them with the spirit of wonder and awe in your presence.

We ask this through Christ our Lord. Amen.

---

B. *Now close your eyes and remember the various parts of the whole celebration—gathering, the lighting of the fire, entering the church, and the whole celebration.*

C. *When you have finished recalling these events, look at the list below. Take your time thinking about each event. Become aware of how you felt as you remember people, music, light, darkness, smells, sounds, and touch. Write down as many feelings, images, and experiences as arise in your memory.*

The lighting of the fire

Baptism, Confirmation, and reception into the Church

Stories of faith: God's Word

The Eucharistic Prayer and eating and drinking Christ's Body and Blood with the community

D. *When you have finished writing about your experience, complete the following open-ended sentences:*

1. At the Easter Vigil my most powerful experience(s) of God's presence was (were) . . .

2. As a person fully initiated into the mysteries of the Catholic faith,

I am empowered by . . .

I believe in . . .

I will proclaim . . .

I will respond by . . .

I pray that . . .

# Treasures of the Catholic Tradition

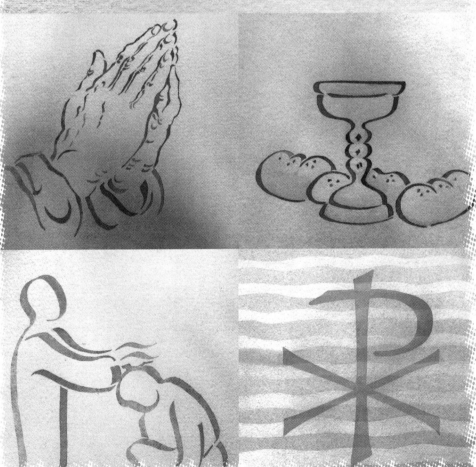

# Traditional Prayers

## Sign of the Cross

In the name of the Father
and of the Son
and of the Holy Spirit,
as it was in the beginning
is now, and ever shall be world without end.
Amen.

## Lord's Prayer

Our Father, who art in heaven,
hallowed be thy name;
thy kingdom come,
thy will be done
on earth as it is in heaven.
Give us this day our daily bread,
and forgive us our trespasses,
as we forgive those who trespass against us;
and lead us not into temptation,
but deliver us from evil.

## Hail Mary

Hail, Mary, full of grace,
the Lord is with thee.
Blessed art thou among women
and blessed is the fruit of thy womb, Jesus.
Holy Mary, Mother of God,
pray for us sinners,
now and at the hour of our death.
Amen.

# GLORY BE

Glory be to the Father
and to the Son
and to the Holy Spirit,
as it was in the beginning
is now, and ever shall be world without end.
Amen.

# APOSTLES' CREED

I believe in God,
the Father almighty,
Creator of heaven and earth,
and in Jesus Christ, his only Son, our Lord,
who was conceived by the Holy Spirit,
born of the Virgin Mary,
suffered under Pontius Pilate,
was crucified, died, and was buried;
he descended into hell;
on the third day he rose again from the dead;
he ascended into heaven,
and is seated at the right hand of God the Father almighty;
from there he will come to judge the living and the dead.

I believe in the Holy Spirit,
the holy catholic Church,
the communion of saints,
the forgiveness of sins,
the resurrection of the body,
and life everlasting. Amen.

# Nicene Creed

I believe in one God,
the Father almighty,
maker of heaven and earth,
of all things visible and invisible.

I believe in one Lord Jesus Christ,
the Only Begotten Son of God,
born of the Father before all ages.
God from God, Light from Light,
true God from true God,
begotten, not made, consubstantial with the Father;
through him all things were made.
For us men and for our salvation
he came down from heaven,
and by the Holy Spirit was incarnate of the Virgin Mary,
and became man.

For our sake he was crucified under Pontius Pilate,
he suffered death and was buried,
and rose again on the third day
in accordance with the Scriptures.
He ascended into heaven
and is seated at the right hand of the Father.
He will come again in glory
to judge the living and the dead
and his kingdom will have no end.

I believe in the Holy Spirit, the Lord, the giver of life,
who proceeds from the Father and the Son,
who with the Father and the Son is adored and glorified,
who has spoken through the prophets.

I believe in one, holy, catholic and apostolic Church.
I confess one Baptism for the forgiveness of sins
and I look forward to the resurrection of the dead
and the life of the world to come. Amen.

# THE MYSTERIES OF THE ROSARY

*THE JOYFUL MYSTERIES* (prayed on Mondays, Thursdays, and the Sundays of Advent)
1. The Annunciation—The messenger of God announces to Mary that she is to be the Mother of God. (Humility)
2. The Visitation—Mary visits and helps her cousin Elizabeth. (Charity)
3. The Nativity—Mary gives birth to Jesus in a stable in Bethlehem. (Poverty)
4. The Presentation in the Temple—Jesus is presented in the Temple, according to Jewish law. (Obedience)
5. The Finding of the Child Jesus After Three Days in the Temple—Jesus is found in the Temple speaking with authority to the rabbis. (Piety)

*THE LUMINOUS MYSTERIES* (prayed on Thursdays)
1. The Baptism at the Jordan—God the Father proclaims Jesus as his beloved Son after John baptizes Jesus in the Jordan River. (Openness to the Holy Spirit)
2. The Miracle at Cana—Jesus changes the water into wine upon the request of Mary. (Fidelity)
3. The Proclamation of the Kingdom and the Call to Conversion—Jesus proclaims the coming of the Kingdom. (Repentance)
4. The Transfiguration—Jesus is transfigured before Peter, James and John while praying on a mountain. (Desire for holiness)
5. The Institution of the Eucharist—Jesus institutes the Eucharist as his Body and Blood for the Salvation of all. (Adoration)

*THE SORROWFUL MYSTERIES* (prayed on Tuesdays, Fridays, and the Sundays of Lent)
1. The Agony in the Garden—Jesus undergoes his agony in the Garden of Gethsemane. (Contrition)
2. The Scourging at the Pillar—Jesus is scourged at the pillar of the Roman courtyard. (Purity)
3. The Crowning with Thorns—Jesus is mocked as the king of the Jews and crowned with thorns. (Courage)
4. The Carrying of the Cross—Jesus carries the Cross to Calvary. (Patience)
5. The Crucifixion and Death—Jesus dies on the Cross for our sins. (Self-denial)

*THE GLORIOUS MYSTERIES* (prayed on Wednesdays, Saturdays, and remaining Sundays of the year)

1. The Resurrection—Jesus rises from the dead on the third day as he promised. (Faith)
2. The Ascension—Jesus ascends into Heaven to sit at the right hand of the Father. (Hope)
3. The Descent of the Holy Spirit at Pentecost—The Holy Spirit comes to the Apostles, Mary, and all the followers gathered in the Upper Room on Pentecost. (Love)
4. The Assumption of Mary—Mary, the Mother of Jesus, is taken into Heaven. (Eternal happiness)
5. The Crowning of the Blessed Virgin as Queen of Heaven and Earth—Mary is crowned queen of Heaven and Earth. (Devotion to Mary)

## HOW TO PRAY THE ROSARY

The complete rosary is composed of twenty decades, but it is divided into four distinct parts, each containing five decades. The first part consists of five joyful events in the life of Jesus and Mary, the second part recalls five sorrowful events, the third part considers five glorious events and the last recalls the luminous events in Jesus' life.

We begin by making the Sign of the Cross. Then recalling each event, we say the Lord's Prayer, ten Hail Marys, and the Glory Be. This completes one decade, and we say all the other decades in the same manner, meditating on a different event during each decade. At the end of the rosary, the Hail, Holy Queen may be recited.

The events (mysteries) of the rosary are scenes from the life of Jesus and Mary. By meditating on these sublime truths we come to a better understanding of our religion: the Incarnation of the Lord, the Redemption, and the Christian life, present and future.

# MEMORARE

Remember, O most gracious Virgin Mary, that never was it known that anyone who fled to your protection, implored your help, or sought your intercession was left unaided. Inspired by this confidence, I fly unto you, O Virgin of virgins, my mother; to you do I come, before you I stand, sinful and sorrowful. O Mother of the Word Incarnate, despise not my petitions, but in your mercy hear and answer me. Amen.

# Morning Offering

O Jesus, through the Immaculate Heart of Mary, I offer You all my prayers, works, and sufferings of this day. For all the intentions of your Sacred Heart. In union with the Holy Sacrifice of the Mass throughout the world. In reparation for all my sins. For the intentions of all our associates, and, in particular, for the intention of our Holy Father for this month. Amen.

# Act of Faith

O my God, I firmly believe that you are one God in three divine Persons, Father, Son, and Holy Spirit; I believe that your divine Son became man and died for our sins, and that he will come to judge the living and the dead. I believe these and all the truths which the Holy Catholic Church teaches, because you revealed them, who can neither deceive nor be deceived.

# Act of Hope

O my God, relying on your infinite goodness and promises, I hope to obtain pardon of my sins, the help of your grace, and life everlasting, through the merits of Jesus Christ, my Lord and Redeemer.

# Act of Love

O my God, I love you above all things, with my whole heart and soul, because you are all good and worthy of all my love. I love my neighbor as myself for the love of you. I forgive all who have injured me and I ask pardon of all whom I have injured.

# Act of Contrition

My God,
I am sorry for my sins with all my heart.
In choosing to do wrong
and failing to do good,
I have sinned against you
whom I should love above all things.
I firmly intend, with your help,
to do penance,
to sin no more,
and to avoid whatever leads me to sin.
Our Savior Jesus Christ
suffered and died for us.
In his name, my God, have mercy.

# EXAMINATION OF CONSCIENCE

How have I shown my love for God and others today?
Do I make an effort to address God regularly in prayer?
How am I aware of others—my family, friends, coworkers?
    Do I hold them in proper esteem?
Am I kind and fair in my relationships with others at home,
    at work, at church, everywhere?
Am I generous and giving or are my possessions of greater importance
    than my relationships?
Do I respect the things I own and the things of others?
Am I consistently honest with others?
Am I careful with their property and their reputations?
Do I worship God by going to Mass and taking an active part
    in the celebration?

# PRAYER BEFORE A CRUCIFIX

Good and gentle Jesus,
I kneel before you.
I see and I ponder your five wounds.
My eyes behold what David prophesied about you:
"They have pierced my hands and feet;
they have counted all my bones."

Engrave on me this image of yourself.
Fulfill the yearnings of my heart:
give me faith, hope, and love,
repentance for my sins,
and true conversion of life.
Amen.

# Grace before Meals

Bless us, O Lord, and these thy gifts,
which we are about to receive from thy bounty,
through Christ our Lord. Amen.

# Grace after Meals

We give thee thanks, for all thy benefits, almighty God,
who lives and reigns forever. Amen.

# The Divine Praises

Blessed be God.
Blessed be his holy name.
Blessed be Jesus Christ, true God and true man.
Blessed be the name of Jesus.
Blessed be his most Sacred Heart.
Blessed be his most precious Blood.
Blessed be Jesus in the most holy Sacrament of the altar.
Blessed be the Holy Spirit, the Paraclete.
Blessed be the great Mother of God, Mary most holy.
Blessed be her holy and Immaculate Conception.
Blessed be her glorious Assumption.
Blessed be the name of Mary, Virgin and Mother.
Blessed be Saint Joseph, her most chaste spouse.
Blessed be God in his angels and in his saints.

# THE JESUS PRAYER

Jesus

Lord Jesus,
have mercy on me,
a sinner.    (Byzantine Daily Worship)

Lord Jesus Christ,
Son of God,
have mercy upon me.    (Traditional Orthodox)

Lord Jesus,
Son of God,
have mercy on me,
a sinner.    (Rite of Penance)

Lord, have mercy.
  Christ, have mercy.
Lord, have mercy.    (Order of Mass)


# CONFITEOR

I confess to almighty God
and to you, my brothers and sisters,
that I have greatly sinned,
in my thoughts and in my words,
in what I have done, and in what I have failed to do,
through my fault, through my fault,
through my most grievous fault;
therefore I ask blessed Mary ever-Virgin,
all the Angels and Saints,
and you, my brothers and sisters,
to pray for me to the Lord our God.

# Prayer to the Holy Spirit

*Verse:*    Come, Holy Spirit, fill the hearts of your faithful.
*Response:*   And kindle in them the fire of your love.
*Verse:*    Send forth your Spirit and they shall be created.
*Response:*   And you will renew the face of the earth.

Let us pray.

Lord,
by the light of the Holy Spirit
you have taught the hearts of your faithful.
In the same Spirit
help us to relish what is right
and always rejoice in your consolation.

We ask this through Christ our Lord.
*Response:*   Amen.

# Prayer to Our Guardian Angel

Angel of God,
my guardian dear,
to whom God's love commits me here,
ever this day be at my side,
to light and guard, to rule and guide.
Amen.

# Anima Christi

Soul of Christ, sanctify me.
Body of Christ, heal me.
Blood of Christ, drench me.
Water from the side of Christ, wash me.
Passion of Christ, strengthen me.

Good Jesus, hear me.

In your wounds shelter me.
From turning away keep me.
From the evil one protect me.
At the hour of my death call me.
Into your presence lead me,
to praise you with all your saints
for ever and ever.
Amen.

# Stations of the Cross

1. Jesus is condemned to death.
2. Jesus accepts his cross.
3. Jesus falls the first time.
4. Jesus meets his mother.
5. Simon helps Jesus carry the cross.
6. Veronica wipes the face of Jesus.
7. Jesus falls the second time.
8. Jesus meets the women.
9. Jesus falls the third time.
10. Jesus is stripped of his clothes.
11. Jesus is nailed to the cross.
12. Jesus dies on the cross.
13. Jesus is taken down from the cross.
14. Jesus is placed in the tomb.

# SALVE REGINA

Hail, holy Queen, Mother of mercy:
Hail, our life, our sweetness and our hope.
To you do we cry, poor banished children of Eve.
To you do we send up our sighs,
mourning and weeping in this valley of tears.
Turn, then, most gracious advocate,
your eyes of mercy toward us;
and after this our exile
show unto us the blessed fruit of your womb, Jesus.
O clement, O loving, O sweet Virgin Mary.

# MY QUEEN, MY MOTHER

My Queen, my Mother, I give myself entirely to you; and to show my devotion to you I consecrate to you this day my eyes, my ears, my mouth, my heart, my whole being without reserve. Wherefore, dear Mother, as I am your own, keep me and guard me as your property and possession. Amen.

# THE ANGELUS

Verse: The Angel of the Lord declared unto Mary,
Response: And she conceived of the Holy Spirit.
Hail Mary. . . .

Verse: Behold the handmaid of the Lord.
Response: Be it done unto me according to your Word.
Hail Mary. . . .

Verse: And the Word was made flesh,
Response: And dwelt among us.
Hail, Mary. . . .

Verse: Pray for us, O holy Mother of God,
Response: that we may be made worthy of the promises of Christ.

Let us pray. Pour forth, we beseech you, O Lord, your grace into our hearts: that we, to whom the Incarnation of Christ your son was made known by the message of an Angel, may by his Passion and Cross be brought to the glory of his Resurrection. Through the same Christ our Lord. Amen.

## PRAYER OF SAINT FRANCIS (PEACE PRAYER)

Lord, make me an instrument of your peace:
where there is hatred, let me sow love;
where there is injury, pardon;
where there is doubt, faith;
where there is despair, hope;
where there is darkness, light;
where there is sadness, joy.

O divine Master, grant that I may not so much seek
to be consoled as to console,
to be understood as to understand,
to be loved as to love.

For it is in giving that we receive,
it is in pardoning that we are pardoned,
it is in dying that we are born to eternal life.
Amen.

# THE ROAD AHEAD

My Lord God, I have no idea where I am going. I do not see the road ahead of me. I cannot know for certain where it will end. Nor do I really know myself, and the fact that I think that I am following your will does not mean that I am actually doing so. But I believe that the desire to please you does in fact please you. And I hope I have that desire in all that I am doing. I hope that I will never do anything apart from that desire. And I know that if I do this, you will lead me by the right road though I may know nothing about it. Therefore will I trust you always though I may seem to be lost and in the shadow of death. I will not fear, for you are ever with me, and you will never leave me to face my perils alone.

This prayer of Thomas Merton is taken from *Thoughts in Solitude.* Copyright © 1956, 1958 by Our Lady of Gethsemani.

# PRAYER OF BLESSED CHARLES DE FOUCAULD

Father, I abandon myself into your hands;
Do with me what you will,
Whatever you may do, I thank you;
I am ready for all, I accept all,
Let only your will be done in me,
And in all your creatures—
I wish no more than this, O Lord.
Therefore will I trust you always
though I may seem to be lost
and in the shadow of death.
I will not fear, for you are ever with me,
and will never leave me to face my perils alone.

# PRAYER OF SAINT IGNATIUS LOYOLA

Take, Lord, and receive
    all my liberty, my memory,
    my understanding, and my entire will,
        all that I have and possess.
You have given all to me.
To you, Lord, I return it.
All is yours.
    Dispose of it wholly according to your will.
Give me your love and your grace,
    for this is enough for me.

# PRAYER OF SAINT AUGUSTINE

## From the *Confessions*

Late have I loved you,
O beauty ever ancient, ever new!
Late have I loved you.

And behold, you were within,
and I without,
and without I sought you.
And deformed,
I ran after those forms of beauty you have made.

You were with me,
and I was not with you,
those things held me back from you,
things whose only being
was to be in you.

You called; you cried;
and you broke through my deafness.
You flashed; you shone;
and you chased away my blindness,
you became fragrant;
and I inhaled and sighed for you,
I tasted,
and now hunger and thirst for you,
You touched me;
and I burned for your embrace.

# FROM THE *B*REASTPLATE OF SAINT PATRICK

*I* arise today
through God's strength to pilot me,
God's might to uphold me,
God's wisdom to guide me,
God's eye to look before me,
God's ear to hear me,
God's hand to guard me,
God's way to lie before me,
God's shield to protect me,
God's hosts to save me
from the snares of the devil.

# *P*RAYER OF POPE SAINT JOHN XXIII

*O* Lord,
Do not let us turn into "broken cisterns,"
that can hold no water.
Do not let us be so blinded by the enjoyment
of the good things of earth
that our hearts become insensible to the
cry of the poor, of the sick,
of orphaned children
and of those innumerable brothers (and sisters) of ours
who lack the necessary minimum
to eat, to clothe their nakedness, and to gather their family
together under one roof.

# PRAYER OF SAINT ANSELM

O Lord, my God,
teach my heart where and how to seek you,
where and how to find you.

O Lord,
you are my God
and you are my Lord,
and I have never seen you.

You have made me and remade me,
and you have bestowed on me
all the good things I possess,
and still I do not know you.
I have not yet done that for which I was made.

Teach me to seek you,
for I cannot seek you
unless you teach me
or find you
unless you show yourself to me.

Let me seek you in my desire,
let me desire you in my seeking.
Let me find you by loving you.
Let me love you when I find you.

# PRAYER OF SAINT CHRISTOPHER

Father, grant that I may be a bearer of Christ Jesus, your Son.
Allow me to warm the often cold, impersonal scene of modern life
    with your burning love.
Strengthen me by Your Holy Spirit to carry out my mission
of changing the world or some definite part of it for the better.
Despite my lamentable failures,
bring home to me that my advantages are your blessings to be
    shared with others.
Make me more energetic in setting right what I find wrong with
    the world
instead of complaining about it.
Nourish in me a practical desire to build up rather than tear
    down,
to reconcile instead of polarize,
to go out on a limb rather than crave security.
Never let me forget that it is far better to light one candle than to
    curse the darkness,
and to join my light, one day, with yours. Amen.

# PRAYER OF SAINT FRANCIS DE SALES

Have no fear for what tomorrow may bring.
The same loving God who cares for you today
will take care of you tomorrow and every day.
God will either shield you from suffering
or give you unfailing strength to bear it.
Be at peace, then,
and put aside all anxious thoughts and imaginations.

# PRAYER OF MARY STUART, QUEEN OF SCOTLAND

Keep us, O Lord, from all pettiness.
Let us be large in thought, in word, and in deed.
Let us be done with fault-finding, and leave off all self-seeking.
May we put away all pretense and meet each other,
Face to face, without self-pity, and without prejudice.
May we never be hasty in judgment, and always generous.

Let us take time for all things.
Make us grow calm, serene, and gently.
Teach us to put into action our better impulses,
Straight forward and unafraid.
Grant that we may realize that it is the little things of life
That create differences,
That in the big things of life we are as one.
And, O Lord God, let us not forget to be kind. Amen.

# PRAYER OF JOHN CARDINAL NEWMAN

God has created me to do Him some definite service.
He has committed some work to me
Which He has not committed to another.

I have my mission,
I may never know it in this life,
But I shall be told it in the next.

I am a link in a chain,
A bond of connection between persons.
He has not created me for naught.

I shall do good—I shall do His word.
I shall be an angel of peace,
A preacher of truth in my own place while not intending it,
If I do but keep his commandments.

Therefore I will trust Him.
Whatever I am, I can never be thrown away.
If I am in sickness, my sickness may serve Him,
In perplexity, my perplexity may serve Him,
If I am in sorrow, my sorrow may serve him.

He does nothing in vain.

He knows what He is about;
He may take away my friends.
He may throw me among strangers,
He may make me feel desolate, make my spirits sink,
Hide my future from me—still He knows what He is about!

# THEOLOGICAL VIRTUES

Faith, hope, charity

# MORAL VIRTUES

Prudence, justice, fortitude, temperance

# GIFTS OF THE HOLY SPIRIT

Wisdom, understanding, counsel, fortitude, knowledge, piety, fear of the Lord

# FRUITS OF THE HOLY SPIRIT

Charity, joy, peace, patience, kindness, goodness, generosity, gentleness, faithfulness, modesty, self-control, chastity

# THE BEATITUDES

"Blessed are the poor in spirit,
   for theirs is the kingdom of heaven.
Blessed are they who mourn,
   for they will be comforted.
Blessed are the meek,
   for they will inherit the land.
Blessed are they who hunger and thirst for righteousness,
   for they will be satisfied.
Blessed are the merciful,
   for they will be shown mercy.
Blessed are the clean of heart,
   for they will see God.
Blessed are the peacemakers,
   for they will be called children of God.
Blessed are they who are persecuted for the sake of righteousness,
   for theirs is the kingdom of heaven.
Blessed are you when they insult you and persecute you and utter
   every kind of evil against you [falsely] because of me.
   Rejoice and be glad, for your reward is great in heaven.
   Thus they persecuted the prophets who were before you."

*Matthew 5:3–12*

# TEN COMMANDMENTS

1. I am the LORD your God: you shall not have strange gods before me.
2. You shall not take the name of the LORD your God in vain.
3. Remember to keep holy the LORD's Day.
4. Honor your father and your mother.
5. You shall not kill.
6. You shall not commit adultery.
7. You shall not steal.
8. You shall not bear false witness against your neighbor.
9. You shall not covet your neighbor's wife.
10. You shall not covet your neighbor's goods.

# CAPITAL SINS

Pride, avarice, envy, wrath, lust, gluttony, sloth

# SEVEN SACRAMENTS

Baptism, Confirmation, Eucharist, Penance and Reconciliation, Anointing of the Sick, Holy Orders, Matrimony

# PRECEPTS OF THE CHURCH

Assist at Mass on Sundays and holy days of obligation.
Fast and abstain on the days appointed.
Confess your sins at least once a year.
Receive Holy Communion during the Easter season.
Contribute to the support of the Church.
Observe the laws of the Church concerning marriage.

# HOLY DAYS OF OBLIGATION IN THE UNITED STATES

Immaculate Conception of the Blessed Virgin Mary, December 8
The Nativity of the Lord (Christmas), December 25
The Solemnity of Mary, the Holy Mother of God, January 1
The Ascension of the Lord, forty days after Easter (or the Seventh Sunday of Easter)
The Solemnity of the Assumption of the Blessed Virgin Mary, August 15
The Solemnity of All Saints, November 1

# CORPORAL WORKS OF MERCY

Feed the hungry.
Give drink to the thirsty.
Shelter the homeless.
Clothe the naked.
Care for the sick.
Visit prisoners.
Bury the dead.

# SPIRITUAL WORKS OF MERCY

Share knowledge.
Give advice to those who need it.
Comfort those who suffer.
Be patient with others.
Forgive those who hurt you.
Give correction to those who need it.
Pray for others.

# Resources

Anderson, Lorraine, ed. *Sisters of the Earth*. New York: Vintage Books, 1991.

Berry, Wendell. *Collected Poems 1957–1982*. San Francisco: North Point Press, 1985.

Burton-Christie, Douglas. "We Already Have All That We Seek: Prayer as Radical Simplicity." *Weavings: A Journal of the Christian Spiritual Life*, May/June 1995, pp. 19–21.

Canham, Elizabeth J. "Clutch Clinic." *Weavings: A Journal of the Christian Spiritual Life*, March/April 1997, pp. 32–33.

Cape, Jonathan, trans. *An Interrupted Life: The Diaries of Etty Hillesum 1941–43*. New York: Washington Square Press, 1983.

Carroll, L. Patrick, S.J. *Where God May Be Found*. New York: Paulist Press, 1994.

Chittister, Joan, OSB. "Wait: Listen to Advent's Lesson." *National Catholic Reporter*, 19 December 1986, p. 10.

Clarke, Thomas E., S.J. "Fear and Anger on Our Side." *Weavings: A Journal of the Christian Spiritual Life*, May/June 1997, pp. 24–26.

_____. "The Mixed Blessing of Community." *Weavings: A Journal of the Christian Spiritual Life*, September/October 1996, pp. 20–21.

Curzon, David, ed. *The Gospels in Our Image: An Anthology of Twentieth-Century Poetry Based on Biblical Texts*. New York: Harcourt Brace & Company, 1995.

Dillard, Annie. *Pilgrim at Tinker Creek*. New York: Harper & Row, 1974.

Donnelly, Doris. "Advent, The Most Difficult Season." *Origins*, September 10, 1987, p. 206.

Durka, Gloria. *Praying with Julian of Norwich*. Winona, WI: St. Mary's Press, 1989.

Escamilla, Paul Lynd. "Something Bigger Than All of Us: Koinonia, Fruitfulness, and Joy in the Worship of God." *Weavings: A Journal of the Christian Spiritual Life*, July/August 1995, pp. 27–28.

Estés, Clarissa Pinkola. *The Gift of Story: A Wise Tale About What is Enough*. New York: Ballantine Books 1993.

Gire, Ken. *Between Heaven and Earth: Prayers and Reflections That Celebrate an Intimate God*. Harper SanFrancisco, 1997.

Hilsinger, Serena Sue and Byrnes, Lois, eds. *Selected Poems of May Sarton*. New York: W.W. Norton and Company, 1978.

Hooper, Walter, ed. *C. S. Lewis: Readings for Meditation and Reflection*. San Francisco: HarperCollins, 1992.

Johnson, Ann. *Miryam of Nazareth: Woman of Strength and Wisdom*. Notre Dame: Ave Maria Press, 1984.

Johnson, Elizabeth A. *Women, Earth, and Creator Spirit*. New York: Paulist Press, 1993.

Jones, Charles E., ed. *Remember Man*. Notre Dame: Ave Maria Press, 1971.

Jones, W. Paul. "Courage as the Heart of Faith." *Weavings: A Journal of the Christian Spiritual Life*, May/June 1997, pp. 12–13.

Leckey, Dolores R. "Pursuing Paths of Grace." *Weavings: A Journal of the Christian Spiritual Life*, January/February 1996, pp. 23–24.

L'Engle, Madeleine. *A Stone for a Pillow: Journeys with Jacob*. Wheaton, IL: Harold Shaw Publishers, 1986.

Lindbergh, Anne Morrow. *Gift from the Sea*. New York: Vintage Books, Random House, 1955.

Loder, Ted. *Guerrillas of Grace: Prayers for the Battle*. San Diego, CA: LuraMedia, 1984.

Lund, Candida, ed. *In Joy and In Sorrow*. Chicago: Thomas More, 1984.

McDonnell, Thomas P., ed. *Thomas Merton Reader*. Garden City, NY: Doubleday, 1974.

Merton, Thomas. *Conjectures of a Guilty Bystander*. Garden City, NY: Image Books, 1968.

_____. *He Is Risen*. Niles, IL: Argus Communications, 1975.

Moffit, John. "The Pattern." *America,* April 18, 1987, p. 323.

Norris, Kathleen. *The Cloister Walk*. New York: Riverhead Books, 1996.

Nouwen, Henri J. *Gracias! A Latin American Journal*. San Francisco: HarperCollins, 1983.

_____. *Show Me the Way*. New York: Crossroad, 1992.

Prevallet, Elaine M., S.L. "Minding the Call." *Weavings: A Journal of the Christian Spiritual Life,* May/June 1996, pp. 9–10.

Recla, Lawrence. "Now and Again." *Praying,* July/August 1997, p. 27.

Sewell, Marilyn, ed. *Cries of the Spirit: A Celebration of Women's Spirituality*. Boston: Beacon Press, 1991.

Shea, John. *The Hour of the Unexpected*. Allen, TX: Argus Communications, 1977.

Sleevi, Mary Lou. *Sisters and Prophets*. Notre Dame: Ave Maria Press, 1993.

Szews, George R. "Mary and Other Special People Near the Edge." *National Catholic Reporter,* 6 January 1995, p. 9.

Wiederkehr, Macrina. *Seasons of Your Heart*. San Francisco: HarperCollins, 1991.

Wright, Wendy M. "Memories of Now." *Weavings: A Journal of the Christian Spiritual Life,* May/June 1995, pp. 9–10.

_____. "Catherine of Siena." *Weavings: A Journal of the Christian Spiritual Life,* July/August 1997, pp. 9–11.

# Acknowledgments

Scripture excerpts are taken from the *New Revised Standard Version Bible* Copyright © 1993, 1989, by the Division of Christian Education of the National Council of the Churches of Christ in the U.S.A. Used by permission.

The English translation of the *Confiteor* from *The Roman Missal* © 2011, International Committee on English in the Liturgy, Inc. (ICEL); the Prayer before a Crucifix, the Prayer to the Holy Spirit, *Anima Christi,* and the *Angelus* from English translation of *A Book of Prayers* © 1982, ICEL; excerpts from the English translation of *Rite of Christian Initiation of Adults* © 1985, ICEL. All rights reserved.

Berry, Wendell. "Grace." From *Openings.* Copyright © 1967 and renewed 1985 by Wendell Berry, reprinted by permission of Harcourt Brace & Company.

Berry, Wendell. "The Broken Ground," "Breaking," "To Know the Dark." From *Collected Poems 1957–1982.* Copyright © 1984 by Wendell Berry. Published by North Point Press, San Francisco.

Burton-Christie, Douglas. "A World of Infinite Depth." From "We Already Have All That We Seek," *Weavings: A Journal of the Christian Spiritual Life,* May/June 1995. Reprinted by permission of the author.

Canham, Elizabeth. "Seasons of Personal Examination." From *Weavings: A Journal of the Christian Spiritual Life,* March/April 1997. Reprinted by permission of the author.

Carroll, L. Patrick. From *Where God May Be Found* by L. Patrick Carroll, S.J. Copyright © 1994 by the Oregon Province of the Society of Jesus. Used by permission of Paulist Press.

Chittister, Joan. "Wait: Listen to Advent's Lesson." From *National Catholic Reporter,* December 19, 1986. Reprinted by permission of the publisher.

Clarke, Thomas E. "The Roots of Interpersonal and Social Conflict." From *Weavings: A Journal of the Christian Spiritual Life,* volume XI, number 5, September/October 1996. Reprinted by permission of the author.

Clarke, Thomas E. "Fear and Anger Redeemed." From *Weavings: A Journal of the Christian Spiritual Life,* volume XII, number 3, May/June 1997. Reprinted by permission of the author.

Clifton, Lucille. "spring song." From *Good Woman: Poems and a Memoir 1969–1980.* Copyright © 1987 by Lucille Clifton. Reprinted with the permission of BOA Editions, Ltd., 260 East Ave., Rochester NY 14604.

Dillard, Annie. "Spring." From *Pilgrim at Tinker Creek* by Annie Dillard. Copyright © 1974 by Annie Dillard. Reprinted by permission of HarperCollins Publishers, Inc.

Donnelly, Doris. "Advent, the Most Difficult Season." From *Origins*, volume 17, issue 13, September 10, 1987. Reprinted by permission of the author.

Escamilla, Paul L. "Koinonia." From "Something Bigger Than All of Us: Koinonia, Fruitfulness, and Joy in the Worship of God," *Worship: A Journal of the Christian Spiritual Life,* July/August 1995. Reprinted by permission of the author.

Estés, Clarissa Pinkola. Excerpt from *The Gift of Story: A Wise Tale About What is Enough* by Clarissa Pinkola Estés, Ph.D., Copyright © 1993. All performance, derivative, adaptation, musical, audio and recording, illustrative, theatrical, film, pictorial, electronic and all other rights reserved. Reprinted by kind permission of the author, Dr. Estés, and Ballantine Books, a division of Random House, Inc.

Gire, Ken. "The Gale Winds of March." From *Between Heaven and Earth: Prayers and Reflections That Celebrate an Intimate God* by Ken Gire. Copyright © 1997 by Ken Gire. Reprinted by permission of HarperCollins Publishers, Inc.

Harjo, Joy. "Eagle Poem." From *In Mad Love & War* by Joy Harjo. Copyright © 1990 by Joy Harjo, Wesleyan University Press by permission of University Press of New England.

Hillesum, Etty. "An Interrupted Life." From *An Interrupted Life* by Etty Hillesum, translated by Arno Pomerans. English translation Copyright © 1983 by Jonathan Cape Ltd. Copyright © 1981 by De Haan/Uniboek b.v., Bussum. Reprinted by permission of Pantheon Books, a division of Random House, Inc.

Johnson, Ann. "Pentecost." From *Miryam of Nazareth* by Ann Johnson. Copyright © 1984 by Ave Maria Press, Notre Dame, IN. Used with permission of the publisher.

Johnson, Elizabeth. "Water and the Spirit," "Contemplation and Communion." From *Women, Earth, and Creator Spirit* by Elizabeth A. Johnson. Copyright © 1993 by Saint Mary's College, Notre Dame, IN. Used by permission of Paulist Press.

Jones, W. Paul. "The Escape from Courage." From *Weavings: A Journal of the Spiritual Life,* May/June 1997. Used by permission of the author.

Kenyon, Jane. "Briefly It Enters, and Briefly Speaks." Copyright © 1996 by the Estate of Jane Kenyon. Reprinted from *Otherwise: New & Selected Poems* with the permission of Graywolf Press, Saint Paul, MN.

Kipling, Rudyard. "The Sons of Martha." From *Rudyard Kipling's Verse: Definitive Edition.* Reprinted courtesy of Bantam Doubleday Dell.

Leckey, Dolores. "Walking with Jesus." Reprinted by permission of the author. The Tolkien quote is from *The Fellowship of the Ring* by J.R.R. Tolkien. Copyright © 1954, 1965 by J.R.R. Tolkien. Copyright © renewed 1982 by Christopher R. Tolkien, Michael H.R. Tolkien, John F.R. Tolkien and Priscilla M.A.R. Tolkien. Reprinted by permission of Houghton Mifflin Co. All rights reserved.

L'Engle, Madeleine. "The Butterfly Effect." From *The Irrational Season* by Madeleine L'Engle. Copyright © 1977 by Crosswills Ltd. Reprinted by permission of HarperCollins Publishers, Inc.

Levertov, Denise. "The Fountain." From *Poems 1960–1967.* Copyright © 1961 by Denise Levertov. Reprinted by permission of New Directions Publishing Corp.

Lewis, C.S. "The Divorce of Heaven and Hell." From *The Great Divorce.* Copyright © 1946 by C.S. Lewis. Reprinted by permission of Harper Collins Publishers.

Lewis, C.S. "Forgiving and Excusing," from "On Forgiveness." "The Second Coming," from "The World's Last Night." From *Fern-seed and Elephants.* Copyright © 1975 by C.S. Lewis. Reprinted by permission of Harper Collins Publishers.

Lindberg, Anne M. "Moon Shell," "The Winged Life." From *Gift from the Sea* by Anne Morrow Lindbergh. Copyright © 1955, 1975, and renewed 1983 by Anne Morrow Lindbergh. Reprinted by permission of Pantheon Books, a division of Random House, Inc.

Loder, Ted. "Help Me to Believe in Beginnings," "I Need to Breathe Deeply." From *Guerrillas of Grace* by Ted Loder. Copyright © 1984 by Ted Loder. Reprinted by permission of Innisfree Press, Philadelphia, PA.

McLellan, Joseph. "Thou Art Dust." From *Remember Man* by Joseph McLellan. Copyright © 1971 by Joseph McLellan. Reprinted by permission of Ave Maria Press, Notre Dame, IN.

Merton, Thomas. "He Is Risen." From *He Is Risen* by Thomas Merton. Copyright © 1975 by Argus Communications. Used by permission of the publisher.

Merton, Thomas. "Realization." From *Conjectures of a Guilty Bystander* by Thomas Merton. Copyright © 1966 by The Abbey of Gethsemani. Used by permission of Doubleday, a division of Bantam Doubleday Dell Publishing Group, Inc.

Merton, Thomas. "Seeds of Contemplation." From *Seeds of Contemplation.* Copyright © 1949 by Our Lady of Gethsemani Abbey. Reprinted by permission of New Directions Publishing Corp.

Merton, Thomas. "Prayer." From *Thoughts in Solitude* by Thomas Merton. Copyright © 1956, 1958 by the Abbey of Our Lady of Gethsemani. Reprinted by permission of Farrar, Straus & Giroux.

Moffitt, John. "The Pattern." From the prayers of John Moffitt, #9806, Special Collections Department, University of Virginia Library. Reprinted by permission of the University of Virginia Library.

Norris, Kathleen. "At Last, Her Laundry's Done." From *The Cloister Walk.* Copyright © 1996 by Kathleen Norris. Used with permission of Riverhead Books.

Nouwen, Henri. "Advent Hope." From *Gracias! A Latin American Journal* by Henri J. M. Nouwen. Copyright © 1983 by Henri J. M. Nouwen. Reprinted by permission of HarperCollins Publishers, Inc.

Pasternak, Boris. "The Miracle." Translation by Nina Kossman.

Prevallet, Elaine M., S.L. "Minding the Call." From *Weavings: A Journal of the Spiritual Life,* May/June 1996. Used by permission of the author.

Recla, Lawrence. "Now and Again." From *Praying,* July/August 1997. Used by permission of the author.

Sarton, May. "Gestalt at Sixty." From *Selected Poems of May Sarton* by Serena Sue Hilsinger and Lois Brynes, eds. Copyright © 1972 by May Sarton. Reprinted by permission of W. W. Norton & Company, Inc.

Sexton, Anne. "Welcome Morning." From *The Awful Rowing Toward God* by Anne Sexton. Copyright © 1975 by Loring Conant, Jr., Executor of the Estate of Anne Sexton. Reprinted by permission of Houghton Mifflin Company. All rights reserved.

Shea, John. "Sharon's Christmas Prayer." From *The Hour of the Unexpected* by John Shea. Copyright © 1977 by John Shea. Reprinted by permission of the publisher, Thomas More, Allen, TX.

Sleevi, Mary Lou. "The Seeker." From *Sisters and Prophets* by Mary Lou Sleevi. Copyright © 1993 by Mary Lou Sleevi. Used with permission of Ave Maria Press, Notre Dame, IN.

Szews, George. "Mary." From *National Catholic Reporter,* January 6, 1995. Reprinted by permission of the publisher.

Vallejo, Cesar. "Our Daily Bread." From *Neruda and Vallejo: Selected Poems*, ed. Robert Bly. Beacon Press, Boston, 1971. Reprinted by permission of Robert Bly.

Wiederkehr, Macrina. "Fire on the Earth," "The Road of Trust," "The Prayer of One Ready for Birth," "The Prayer of One Bursting with Life." From *Seasons of Your Heart: Prayers and Reflections* by Macrina Wiederkehr. Copyright © 1991 by Macrina Wiederkehr. Reprinted by permission of HarperCollins Publishers, Inc.

Wood, Nancy. "My Help Is in the Mountain." From *Hollering Sun.* Copyright © 1972 by Nancy Wood. Published by Simon & Schuster. Reprinted by permission of the author. All rights reserved.

Wright, Wendy M. "Catherine of Siena," "Saint Augustine's Confessions." From "Memories of Now," *Weavings: A Journal of the Christian Spiritual Life,* May/June 1995. Reprinted by permission of the author.